AF439139

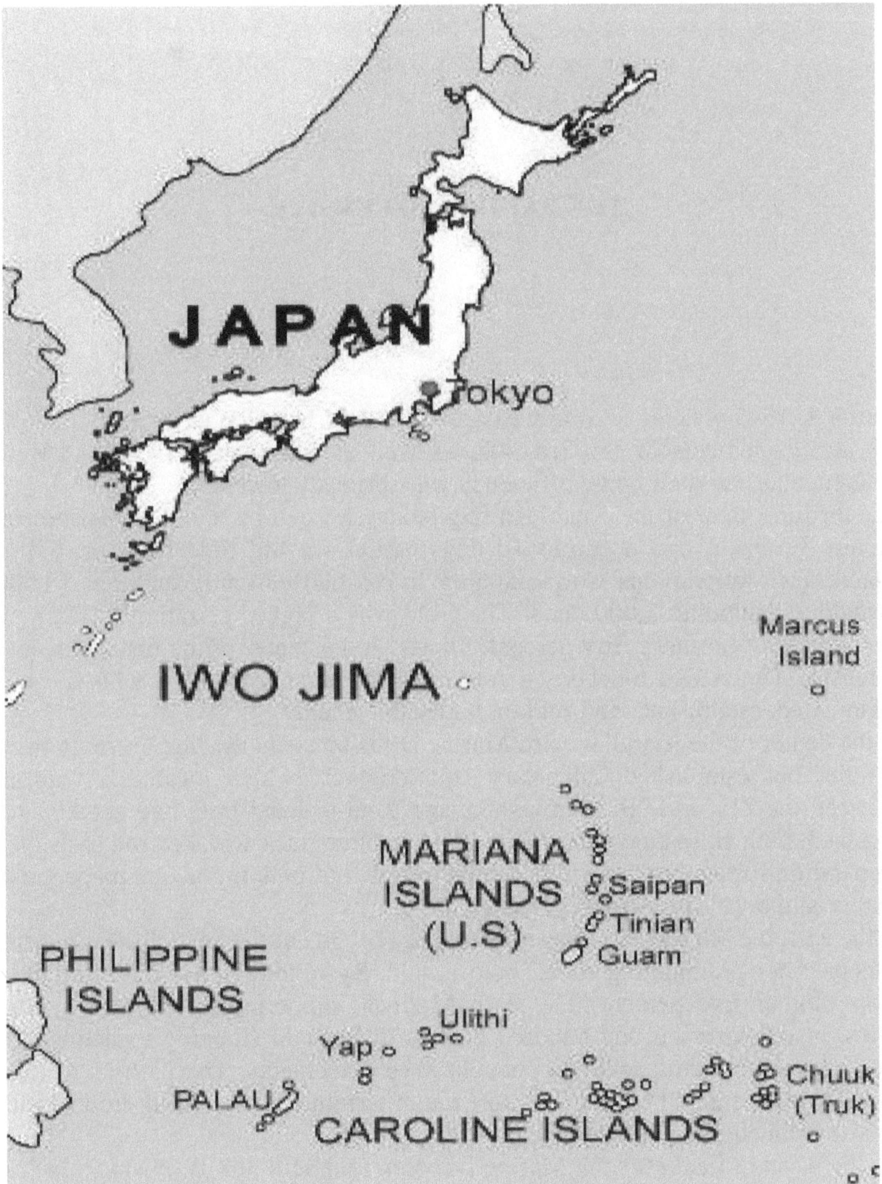

JAPAN
Tokyo
IWO JIMA
Marcus Island
MARIANA ISLANDS (U.S)
Saipan
Tinian
Guam
PHILIPPINE ISLANDS
Ulithi
Yap
PALAU
CAROLINE ISLANDS
Chuuk (Truk)

THE PACIFIC OFFENSIVE

March 4, 1945 was the second week of the Allied invasion of Iwo Jima. Now, the attack elements of the 3rd, 4th, as well as 5th Marine Divisions were drained, and also their battle efficiency was seriously lowered.

The thrilling sight of the American flag being elevated by the 28th Marines on Mount Suribachi had occurred 10 days earlier-- a life time back on Sulfur Island. The Amphibious Corps landing forces had currently endured 13,000 casualties, including 3,000 dead. The front was a jagged serration throughout Iwo Jima's fat northern fifty percent. Smack in the center of the main Japanese defenses. The Allied touchdown force had to advance uphill versus a well-regimented, established, and seldom noticeable enemy.

In the center of the island, the 3rd Marine Division spent the night turning back a little, but established, adversary counterattack, which located a void in between the 21st and 9th Marines. Savage hand-to-hand fight had actually set you back both sides heavy casualties. The counterattack wrecked the division's preparation for an early morning breakthrough, but both regiments made gains against stubborn adversary resistance.

In the east, the 4th Marine Division secured Hill 382 at the cost of their combat effectiveness plummeting listed below half. By nightfall, it would certainly drop another five percent. The 24th Marines, supported by flame-throwing tanks, just progressed one hundred backyards prior to stopping to detonate 2 tons of nitroglycerins against opponent cave placements. The 25th as well as 23rd Marines entered one of the most tough terrain yet-- a busted ground with exposure much less than a few feet.

On the western flank, the 5th Marine Division took Hill 362-B (Nishi.Ridge) at the expense of over 500 casualties. They would certainly engaged a considerable enemy pressure throughout the evening. While the opponent assaults did not have sychronisation, exhausted Marines were hardly able to hold them off. The majority of rifle firms were currently at less than half toughness. The division reported the net gain for the day as "practically absolutely nothing.".

The battle took its toll on the opponent garrison. Japanese General Tadamichi Kuribayashi knew his 109th Division had caused hefty casualties on the attacking Marines, yet his losses were equivalent. The Allied capture of the essential hillsides the day prior to refuted him his valued artillery monitoring websites.

Kuribayashi's great chief of artillery, Colonel Chosaku Kaido, had actually been killed. Kuribayashi relocated his command message from the central highlands to a large cave on the northwestern shore. Imperial Headquarters in Tokyo had reached him by radio that mid-day, yet the general remained in no mood for brave unsupported claims. He replied: "Send air as well as naval support, and I will hold the island. Without them, I can not hold.".

That mid-day, the fighters saw a glimpse of Iwo Jima's destiny. Through the overcast skies, a giant silver bombing plane (the largest airplane yet seen), the B-29 "Dinah Might," came in for an emergency situation touchdown on the shabby island airstrip. Allied troops held their breath as the bombing plane swooped in and landed with a thud. Clipping a field telephone pole with its wing as well as rumbling to a stop three feet from completion of the strip.

Pilot Fred Malo and his ten-man staff didn't remain long. Every opponent artilleryman within range intended to bag this reward. Mechanics made hurried field repair work, as well as the sixty-five-ton Super Fortress rushed via a hailstorm of opponent fire, returning to its base on Tinian.

The fight of Iwo Jima raged for one more twenty-two days and declared 11,000 even more Allied casualties as well as the lives of almost the entire Japanese garrison. A colossal and historical fight between 2 well-armed professional pressures. This was the bloodiest and most significant battle in the history of the Marine Corps. Yet after March 4, leaders on both sides believed as to the best end result.

OPERATION DETACHMENT

Iwo Jima was an aquatic landing where assault soldiers saw the worth of the goal. They were finally within a thousand miles of the Japanese homeland-- as well as adding plainly in support of the Allied battle project.

This battle campaign was a brand-new crease on an old style. For forty years, Marines had actually been creating the abilities to confiscate innovative naval bases in support of the fleet. In the Pacific war-- particularly at Tinian, Saipan, and also now Iwo Jima-- they protected innovative airbases to enhance the battle of the Japanese home islands.

Allied forces had waited for the arrival of the B-29s for many years. These long-range bombing planes came to be operational too late for the European Theater--.but they would certainly been striking Japan considering that November 1944 with frustrating results. The issue wasn't the airplanes or the pilots, yet from a little spit of volcanic rock existing halfway throughout the course from Saipan to Tokyo-- Iwo Jima.

Radar on Iwo gave the enemy 2 hrs' advance notification of every B-29 strike. Japanese fighters on Iwo's landing fields would abound as well as harass the unescorted Super Fortresses entering and specifically returning to base. Adversary fighters picked off the B-29s maimed from antiaircraft fire. This triggered the B-29s to fly greater and also with a decreased payload.

The Joint Chiefs made a decision Iwo Jima need to be secured with an Allied landing field constructed there. This would certainly stop Japanese bombing raids and very early caution interceptions. The landing field would certainly use competitor companions with the treacherous parts of the B-29's goals and higher payloads at longer varieties. Iwo Jima in Allied hands would certainly likewise supply emergency situation airfield assistance as well as touchdown for paralyzed B-29s returning from Tokyo as well as secure the Allied flank for the Okinawa intrusion. Admiral Chester Nimitz was provided 3 months to confiscate as well as create Iwo Jima: codename Operation Detachment.

Iwo Jima translates to "Sulfur Island" in Japanese. An ugly, foul- smelling, barren chunk of volcanic rock as well as sand-- not even ten square miles in dimension. According to a Japanese Army policeman: "an island of sulfur, no sparrow, no ingest, no water.".

Much less poetic Marines explained Iwo's resemblance to a pork chop with a 556-foot volcano. Mount Suribachi dominated the southern end of the island and also overlooked all potential landing coastlines. Iwo rose erratically over onto the Motoyama Plateau in the north before dropping greatly off right into the shore and high cliffs and canyons. The northern surface was a protector's dream: an intricate, busted, cave-dotted jungle of stone. Ringed by volcanic steam and a twisted landscape that appeared like a barren moon wild. Greater than one enduring Marine contrasted the spooky silence to something out of Dante's Inferno.

Iwo Jima in 1945 had two compensatory attributes: the armed forces worth of its landing strips and the psychological standing of the island as a historical Japanese belongings. The Allies were currently within Japan's Inner Defense Zone. According to a Japanese policeman: "Iwo Jima is the doorkeeper to the Imperial funding.".

Even with the slowest airplane, Tokyo can be reached in 3 trip hrs from the island. In the Iwo Jima battle, 20,000 Allied and also Japanese troops would be killed during ruthless combating in the last winter season of 1945.

Nobody recommended taking Iwo Jima would certainly be easy. Admiral Nimitz assigned this goal to the very same team that had actually done so well in the earliest amphibious assaults in the Gilberts, Marshalls, and also

Marianas. Admiral Raymond Spruance would applaud the 5th Fleet, Admiral Richmond Kelly Turner would compliment the expeditionary pressures, and also Admiral Harry Hill would certainly regulate the assault pressure.

Operation Detachment needed ruthless army pressure on the enemy and also an accelerated preparation schedule. The Amphibious job pressure preparing to assault Iwo Jima was obtaining pressed on both ends. Admiral Hill seriously needed aquatic ships, shore bombardment vessels, as well as touchdown craft that were presently in operation by General Douglas MacArthur and also his reconquest of the Philippines. Poor weather and stiff adversary resistance incorporated to delay the conclusion of that operation.

The Joint Chiefs reluctantly delayed D-Day on Iwo from January 20 to February 19. The new timetable gave no alleviation for Allied planners. Since of the downpour period, D-Day on Okinawa could be no later on than April 1. This tight timeframe held grim ramifications for the Marine landing pressure.

General Harry Schmidt would command the V Amphibious Corps in the assault. Schmidt's touchdown force included 3 Marine departments (3rd, 4th, and also 5th). Schmidt would have the honor of regulating the biggest US Marine force ever before devoted into a single battle-- a force amounting to over 80,000 troops.

Over fifty percent of these troops were Marine experts from earlier combating in the Pacific. Practical training had prepared new Marines for the tough battle to find. The Iwo Jima assault pressure was probably the most proficient amphibious pressure the world had yet to see.

Two senior Marines shared the limelight on Iwo Jima, as well as background has actually done them both an oppression. General Holland M. Smith, that then commanded the FMF (Fleet Marine Force), was tasked to take part in Operation Detachment as the Expeditionary Troops' Commanding General. This was an unneeded billet. Schmidt had the ranking, experience, staff, and also sources to implement core level duty without being second-guessed.

General Smith was an aquatic pioneer as well as professional of touchdowns in the Gilberts, Marshalls, and also the Marianas. According to him: "My sunlight had virtually established by then. I think they asked me along in case something occurred to Harry Schmidt." Smith would certainly attempt to keep out of Schmidt's method, but his decision to keep the 3rd Marines (Expeditionary Troops Reserve) remains as debatable as it was in 1945.

General Smith proved himself an asset to the Iwo Jima campaign. He was always a voice in the wild in the top-level planning stage. Smith predicted extreme casualties unless even more efficient initial naval bombardment was given. He diverted checking out very important people and the press away from

Schmidt and constantly offered a sensible counterpoint to several of the rosier personnel price quotes. According to Smith: "It's a tough recommendation, that's why we're right here.".

General Schmidt's couple of public declarations left him encumbered anticipating Iwo Jima would be conquered in 10 days. According to post-war accounts, Schmidt resented Smith's regarded duty: "I was the leader of all soldiers on Iwo Jima whatsoever times. Holland Smith never ever had an onshore command message, never provided a single order, as well as never invested a single night onto land. Isn't it vital from a historic point ofview that I commanded the greatest number of Marines ever before to be participated in a solitary action in the whole history of the Marine Corps?".

General Smith did not disagree with those points. While Smith proved to be helpful, Schmidt and his team ought to be credited for planning and also carrying out the challenging and bloody Iwo Jima project.

The V Amphibious Corps' occupation of Iwo Jima was much more remarkable as a result of tough opponent resistance on the island. General Kuribayashi was just one of one of the most fearful opponents of the war. Kuribayashi was a fifth-generation samurai handpicked by the emperor. The Japanese basic mixed battle experience with a cutting-edge mind and an iron will.

Although this would be his only resist US pressures, he learned much about his opponents from earlier solution in the US. Kuribayashi assessed with an unblinking eye the outcomes of previous Japanese efforts to repel Allied invasions of Japanese-held forts.

In addition to the brave unsupported claims, Kuribayashi saw little value in the safeguard- at-the-water's- edge tactics and suicidal banzai strikes that branded Japan's failures from Tarawa to Tinian. Kuribayashi was a realist. He did not anticipate much help from Japan's diminished fleet and flying force. His ideal chance was to fortify Iwo's prohibiting surface with a comprehensive defense, similar to the defense on Peleliu. Kuribayashi would reject coastal defenses, anti-landing, and banzai tactics. Instead, he would certainly wage a battle of attrition: a war of persistence, nerves, as well as time. A delay and also hemorrhage approach. Would the Allied forces despair and also abandon the campaign?

An easy policy this late in the battle was radical to elderly Japanese Navy as well as Army leaders. It was counter to the deeply ingrained Bushido samurai code: a warrior code that saw the protective as just an undesirable hold-up prior to the marvelous offensive can return to-- where the adversary would be destroyed by fire and sword. Imperial Headquarters was nervous. There was evidence of a top-level request for assistance in preventing Allied storm touchdowns from Nazi Germany, whose experience attempting to defend Normandy at the water's side had actually proven devastating.

Japanese command was doubtful. Kuribayashi used his connection to the Emperor to prevent being eased. It was not a total triumph-- the Navy firmly insisted on structure blockhouses and also weapon casements along the obvious landing beaches. Kuribayashi required aid from the finest mining designers and fortification experts in the Empire.

The island favored the defender. Iwo's volcanic sand mixed with cement created an extraordinary concrete for setups. The soft rock was simple to dig. Over fifty percent of the Japanese fort placed their weapons aside as well as grabbed choices and also spades. When Allied bombing planes from the Seventh Air Force started a daily pummeling of the island in early December 1944, Kuribayashi just relocated every little thing underground: weapons, command article, barracks, as well as aid terminals. The design success he accomplished were remarkable. Kuribayashi concealed weapon settings, developed interlocking areas of fire, and also miles of tunnels linking essential defensive placements. Every cave had numerous electrical outlets as well as air flow tubes. One installation inside Mount Suribachi ran seven tales deep. Allied soldiers rarely ran into an online Japanese on the island until the bitter end.

Allied knowledge, helped by records caught in Saipan as well as by a practically everyday flow of airborne monitoring, was puzzled by the Japanese fort's going away act. The image interpreters, using stereoscopic lenses, detailed 775 prospective targets, but all were covered, solidified, as well as covered up. Allied coordinators knew there was no fresh water offered on the island. They saw the rain cisterns as well as understood what the typical regular monthly rains would certainly provide. They determined the opponent fort could not survive under those problems in numbers greater than 12,000 for long. Kuribayashi's force was two times that size. His soldiers had fed on fifty percent supplies of water for months before the fight even began.

Unlike the earlier aquatic assaults on Guadalcanal and Tarawa, Allies would certainly not have a strategic shock on Iwo. Japanese head office believed Iwo would certainly be attacked after the loss of the Marianas. Six months before the battle, Kuribayashi contacted his spouse: "the Americans will most absolutely get into Iwo Jima-- do not look for my return.".

Kuribayashi ruthlessly functioned his men to complete the protective and also training prep work by February 11, 1945. The basic met his objective. Kuribayashi had a mixed pressure of employees and also soldiers, experts as well as seafarers. His artillerymen as well as mortar staffs were the best in the

Empire. Still, he educated and also disciplined them all. Each fighting placement had the commander's "Courageous Battle Vows" plainly posted above the firing apertures. Troops were cautioned to maintain their placement as well as to take ten Marine lives for each Japanese fatality.

General Schmidt released the functional intend on December 23, 1944. This plan had not been elegant. Mount Suribachi towered over the possible touchdown beaches, but the 3,000 backyards of black sand along the southeastern coastline were even more protected from the prevailing winds. It was right here the V Amphibious Corps would certainly come down on D-Day. The 4th Marine Division on the right, the 5th on the left and also the 3rd aside. The key purposes were the reduced airfield and also Suribachi. The assault force would swing into line and attack north shoulder to shoulder.

Preparing for a substantial opponent counterattack on the first night, General Holland Smith claimed: "We invite their counterattack. That's generally when we break their back.".

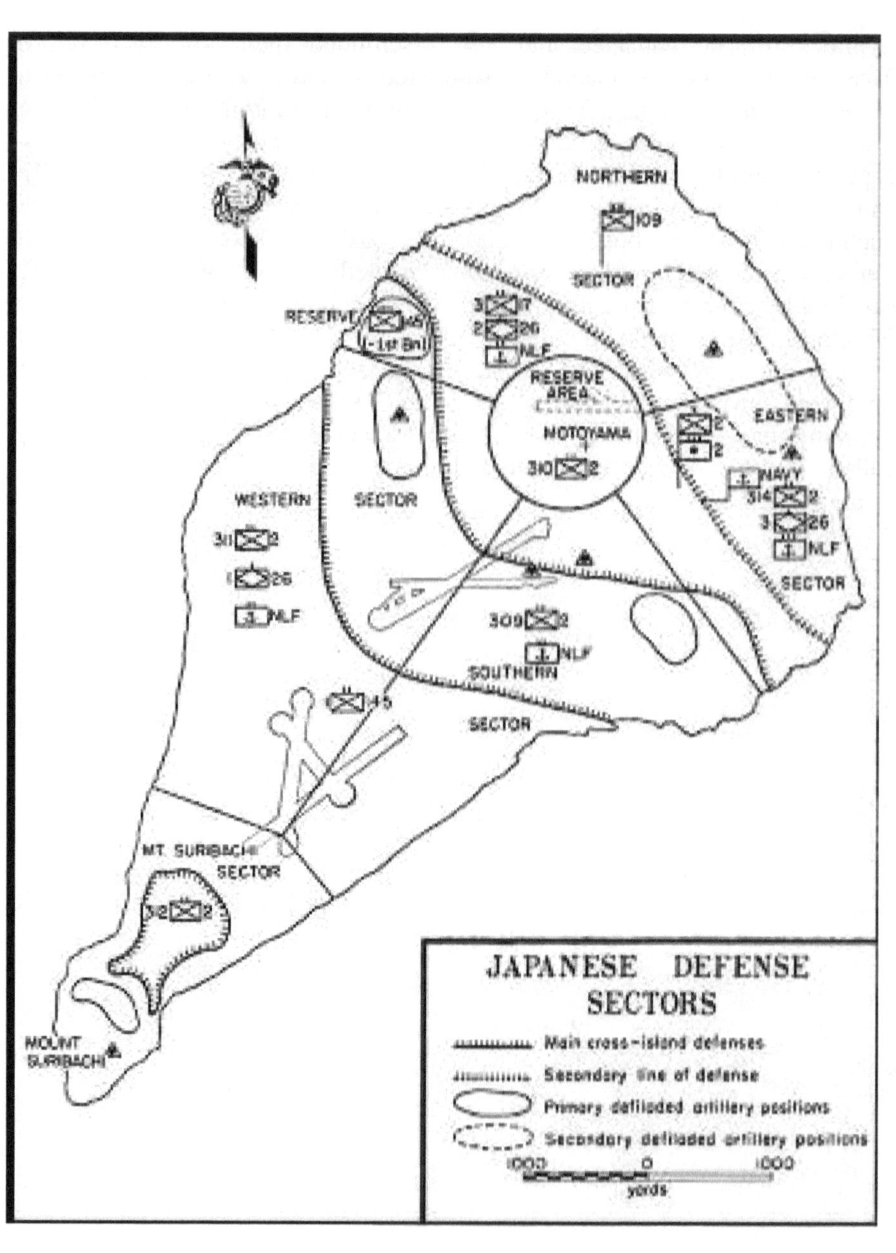

NORTHERN
109
SECTOR
RESERVE
1st Bn
3 7
2 26
NLF
RESERVE
AREA
MOTOYAMA
310 2
2
2
EASTERN
NAVY
314 2
3 26
NLF
WESTERN SECTOR
311 2
26
NLF
309 2
NLF
SECTOR
SOUTHERN
SECTOR
45
MT. SURIBACHI
SECTOR
312 2
MOUNT
SURIBACHI

JAPANESE DEFENSE
SECTORS
Main cross-island defenses
Secondary line of defense
Primary defiladed artillery positions
Secondary defiladed artillery positions
1000   0   1000
yards

KURIBAYASHI'S BIG MISTAKE

The physical separation of the three Marine departments from Hawaii to Guam had no noticeable adverse impact on their training. The efficiency of little units in consolidated arms assaults on fortified placements and also aquatic landing were where it counted most. Each department was well planned for the invasion.

The 3rd Marine Division had simply finished their part in the liberation of Guam. Their area training frequently included energetic combat patrols to root out as well as ruin persistent adversary survivors.

On Maui, the 4th Marine Division planned for their 4th attack touchdown in thirteen months with silent self-confidence. According to Major Fred Karch: "We had a connection of professionals that was unequalled.".

The 5th Marine Division planned for their first combat experience on the big island of Hawaii. The device's freshness would show deceptive. Over fifty percent of the guys and policemans were veterans, including several former Marine Raiders as well as Parachutists that had actually fought in the Solomons. Colonel Don Robertson took command of the 3rd Battalion, 27th Marine Regiment with much less than two weeks prior to embarkation and immediately purchased them into the field for continual live-fire exercises. Their confidence as well as competence persuaded and also amazed Robertson that these Marines were professionals.

Among the veterans preparing to release on Iwo Jima were 2 Medal of Honor recipients from Guadalcanal. Gunnery Sargent John Basilone as well as Colonel Robert Galer. The Marine Corps chose to maintain these distinguished veterans in the US for spirits (bond raising) purposes, yet both men wrangled their back into the battle. Basilone led a gatling gun army and Galer led a brand-new radar system for the Landing Force Air Support. The Guadalcanal experts were surprised at the wealth of amphibious delivery available for Operation Detachment. Admiral Turner regulated 497 ships (140 of these were configured for amphib procedures). This armada was ten times the dimension of the Guadalcanal task force.

There were still issues. Much of the ships and crews were so new that each rehearsal included an unpleasant crash or other crash. New bulldozers (TD-18s) were an inch as well wide for the LCMs. Recently modified M4A3 Sherman containers were so hefty that the LCMs rode with an alarmingly reduced freeboard. The 105mm howitzers overwhelmed the DUKWs (aquatic vehicles) to the point of unseaworthiness. These aspects would quickly show treacherous in Iwo Jima's unforeseeable surf.

Still, the large Allied armada got started as well as started the acquainted move westward healthy, trained, fully equipped, and also extensively supported.

General Kuribayashi had actually gained from the Allied delays of Operation Detachment as a result of the Philippines project. He felt as all set and also ready as possible. When the Allied armada sailed from the Marianas on February 13, he was warned. He deployed one infantry squadron into the lower landing field as well as ordered the mass of his fort right into their appointed combating holes-- to await the unpreventable storm.

2 issues separated the Navy/Marine team as D-Day on Iwo approached. The very first was Admiral Spruance's decision to detach Task Force 58 (the quick attack providers under Admiral Marc Mitscher) to attack tactical targets on Honshu (Main island of Japan) with the synchronised bombardment of Iwo. Marine officers believed a Navy/Air Force rivalry at work: Mitscher's targets were airplane factories that the B-29s had actually missed a few days previously. Mitscher took all eight Marine Corps competitor armadas assigned to the fast service providers, plus the brand-new rapid battlewagons with their 16-inch weapons. While Task Force 58 returned in time to provide fire support on D-Day, they were off once again permanently, 2 days later on.

There was a proceeding disagreement in between elderly Navy and also Marine police officers over the level of the initial marine shooting. Militaries looked at their intelligence records on Iwo Jima and also requested ten days of preparatory fire. The Navy said it did not have the ammo nor the time to spare; 3 days would have to suffice. Generals Smith and also Schmidt pleaded their situation to Admiral Spruance. Their demand was rejected. Admiral Spruance ruled that 3 days of preparatory fire in addition to the daily working carried out by the Seventh Air Force would certainly be good enough to get the job done.

Lieutenant Colonel Don Weller was the Task Force 51 marine gunfire officer, and no man recognized the business better than him. Weller had taken in the Pacific War's lessons well. Specifically the dreadful failures at Tarawa. He said the problem was not the weight of shells and various other quality yet rather the time. The destruction of heavily fortified adversary targets took purposeful as well as pinpoint firing from close range. They needed to be analyzed as well as readjusted by aerial observers. His 7 hundred plus tough targets would require time to knock out-- a lot of time.

Admiral Spruance did not have time to give for strategic, tactical, and logistical factors. Three days of shooting would supply four times the coverings than Tarawa as well as would certainly be one as well as a half time as much delivered against the bigger Saipan. It would certainly have to do.

Iwo's notoriously nasty weather condition as well as solid enemy fortifications dissipated the three-day barrage. According to General William Rogers: "We got around 13 hours with the fire support during the 34 hrs of readily available daytime.".

General Kuribayashi committed his only recognized tactical error throughout this fight. On D minus 2, a force of one-hundred Navy and also Marine frogmen approached the eastern beaches. They were escorted by a loads rocket-firing LCI (Landing Craft Infantry). Kuribayashi believed this was the main assault and also authorized the seaside batteries to open up fire. This exchange was hefty and also warm with the LCIs getting the most awful of it, but the United States cruisers and battleships hurried to blast the sash guns that were unexpectedly disclosed on Suribachi's ideal flank.

That evening, seriously concerned regarding the thousands of Japanese targets untouched by two days of firing, Admiral Turner accredited a "battle council" on his flagship and junked the original plan. He got the gunships to concentrate specifically on beach locations. This was performed with substantial result on D minus 1 and D-Day early morning.

Kuribayashi noted most of the settings the Imperial Navy insisted on.

building along the coastline were ruined-- equally as he anticipated. His main protective force that crisscrossed the Motoyama Plateau remained undamaged. "I wish a heroic battle," Kuribayashi informed his personnel.

The press rundown held the evening prior to D-Day on Admiral Turner's flagship was uncommonly somber. General Holland Smith forecasted hefty casualties: upwards of 15,000, which shocked every person. A guy clad in khakis without a ranking insignia after that dealt with the room and stood. It was the Secretary of the Navy, James Forrestal: "Iwo Jima, like Tarawa, leaves really little option. Except to take it forcibly of arms, by character, and also by guts.".

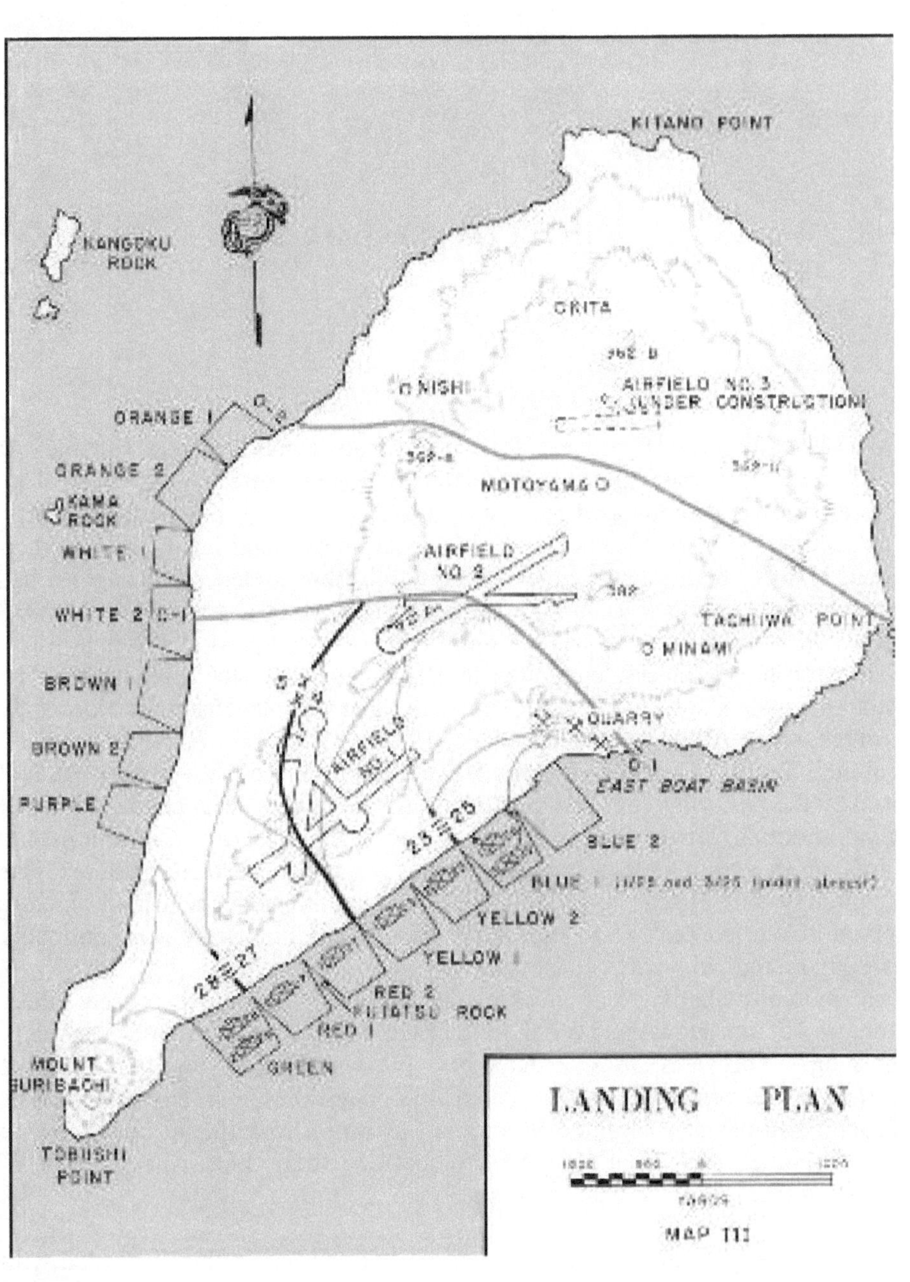

KITANO POINT
KANGOKU ROCK
ORITA
AIRFIELD NO. 3
(UNDER CONSTRUCTION)
NISHI
ORANGE 1
ORANGE 2
KAMA ROCK
MOTOYAMA
WHITE 1
AIRFIELD NO. 2
TACHIIWA POINT
WHITE 2
MINAMI
BROWN 1
BROWN 2
QUARRY
PURPLE
AIRFIELD NO. 1
EAST BOAT BASIN
BLUE 2
BLUE 1
YELLOW 2
YELLOW 1
RED 2
FUTATSU ROCK
RED 1
MOUNT SURIBACHI
GREEN
TOBIISHI POINT
LANDING PLAN
MAP III

D-DAY ON IWO JIMA

On D-Day morning, February 19, Iwo's climate condition were suitable. At 0645, Admiral Turner signaled: "Land the landing pressure."

Shore barrages had engaged the enemy island at close to point-blank variety. Battleships and also cruisers steamed in as close as 1,500 lawns to level their guns against their island targets. Many of these older battlewagons had performed this dangerous mission in other theaters of the war. The Nevada, increased from the filth as well as ruin of Pearl Harbor, led the barrage force. The battleship Arkansas, integrated in 1912, had joined the armada from the Atlantic where she would certainly damaged German placements at Normandy throughout the Allied landing on June 6, 1944.

Colonel "Bucky" Buchanan developed an altered kind of the "rolling battery" used by the pestering gunships versus beachfront targets. This concentration of naval shooting progressed progressively as soldiers landed. Constantly 400 yards to the front. Air watchmans would certainly control the rate. This technology was appealing to the department commanders who had actually served in World War I France. In those days, a moving battery was commonly the only method to break a stalemate.

The amount of shelling was shocking. Admiral Hill later on composed: "there were no appropriate targets for shore barrage continuing to be on D-Day early morning." This was an overstatement. No one denied the fierceness of firepower delivered versus the touchdown coastlines and bordering areas. General Kuribayashi admitted in an analysis report to Imperial headquarters: "we require to reconsider the power of barrage from ships. The violence of opponent barrages is far past summary."

When the job pressure showed up over the horizon, army ships crowded with combat-equipped Marines gazed at the sensational fireworks. The Guadalcanal experts among them enjoyed with grim satisfaction as battlewagons hammered the island. The world had actually come full circle from the dark days of October 1942: when the 1st Marines and also the Cactus Air Force experienced a similar shelling from Japanese battlewagons.

Sailors and also Marines were eager to get their first look of the purpose. Battle contributor John Marquand composed of his first impressions on Iwo: "a silhouette like a sea beast, with a little dead volcano for a head and also the beach location for the neck and a scrubby brownish cliff for the body."

Navy Lieutenant David Susskind wrote his ideas from the bridge of the troopship Mellette: "Iwo Jima was a discourteous and also awful sight. Only a geologist can consider it as well as not be disgusted."

A cosmetic surgeon in the 25th Marines, Lieutenant Mike Keleher wrote: "the marine bombardment had already begun. I saw the orange-yellow flashes as the cruisers, battleships, and also destroyers blew up away at the island with broadsides. We were close to Iwo, similar to the models and pictures we would certainly been examining for weeks. A volcano was on our left and also long level coastlines in a rough, rocky plateau got on our right."

General Clifton Cates examined the island through field glasses from his ship. Each department would certainly land two strengthened programs abreast. From entrusted to right, the beaches were assigned Green, Red, Yellow, and also Blue. The 5th Division would land the 27th as well as 28th Marines on the left flank on Green and also Red Beaches, While the 4th would land the 23rd as well as 25th Marines on the appropriate flank at Blue Beach.

General Schmidt examined the current intelligence records with expanding anxiety and asked for that General Holland Smith reassign the reserve forces. Schmidt desired the 3/21 Marines to change the 26th Marines as the core get and also launch them to the 5th Division. Schmidt pictured the 28th Marines reducing the island in half prior to turning to capture Suribachi. The 25th would certainly scale the rock quarry, functioning as the joint for the entire corps to swing north. The 27th and 23rd Marines would then catch the very first landing field, prior to pivoting north into their assigned areas.

General Cates was concerned about Blue Beach on the appropriate flank. Blue Beach was directly under the observation and fire of suspected enemy placements in the rock quarry. Steep high cliffs outweighed their appropriate flank, while Suribachi controlled the left. The 4th Division figured that the 25th Militaries would certainly have one of the most difficult objective to tackle D-Day. General Cates said: "if I understood the name of the man on the right wing of that team, I 'd advise him for a medal prior to we even arrive."

Iwo Jima was the pinnacle of a forced amphibious touchdown versus a greatly fortified shore. A complex art mastered by the Fifth Fleet through many painstaking campaigns. B-24 bombers from the Seventh Air Force flew in to strike the cigarette smoking island. Spaceship moved in to saturate shore targets. Competitor and assault squadrons from Mitscher's Task Force 58 participated in. While Navy pilots revealed their abilities at battle and strafing, the soldiers started supporting at the sight of F4U Corsairs flown in from Marine fighter squadron 213.

Colonel Vernon McGee was the air police officer for the Expeditionary Troops. He urged this unique show for the guys in the attack waves. "Drag your stomaches on the beach," McGee claimed to the Marine boxers. The F4U Corsairs made an aggressive approach parallel to the island. They streaked reduced over the coastlines as well as savagely strafed opponent targets. The Pacific War location considering that Bougainville maintained ground Marines divided from their air support. According to McGee: "it was the novice many troops had actually ever seen a Marine boxer aircraft, and they were not disappointed."

Not long after the planes left, marine shooting returned to. Shooting carpeted the beach with a crescendo of high eruptive shells. Ship-to-shore activity was underway, an easy thirty-minute run for the LVTs. For Operation Detachment, there were enough LVTs to do the job. Sixty-eight LVT (A) 4 armored amtracs, with snub-nosed 75mm cannons, blew up the method forward with 385 troop filled LVTs complying with close behind. The attack waves crossed the line of departure on schedule and confidently chugged toward the smoking cigarettes beaches.

On Iwo, there was no coral reef or awesome neap tides to fret about. Navy frogmen removed the techniques of mines and tetrahedrons. There was no early secession of fire. The changed rolling barrage was in effect, and no automobiles were lost from opponent fire. Attack waves struck the beaches within 2 mins of H-hour. Opponent viewers watching the dramatization unravel from a cavern on the inclines of Suribachi reported: "At 9 am, numerous hundred landing craft with amphibious containers hurried towards shore like an enormous tidal bore."

Colonel Robert Williams, XO of the 28th Marines, later on wrote: "The landing was a stunning sight to see-- two departments touchdown abreast-- you might see the whole show from the deck of a ship. At this moment, thus far so excellent."

The very first challenge didn't originated from the Japanese, but from the beach as well as its identical terraces. Iwo was a volcano with steep coastlines that greatly dropped off into a narrow as well as terrible surf area. Soft black sand immobilized all wheeled cars and created numerous tracked amphibious automobiles to tummy down and also get stuck.

The following watercraft waves had even more difficulty. They obtained stuck as well when ramps went down and a Jeep or vehicle would drive out.

Plunging waves

would bump the stalled craft prior to they can discharge, loading their sterns
with water as well as sand and broaching them broadside. The coastline
swiftly came to be a salvage yard.

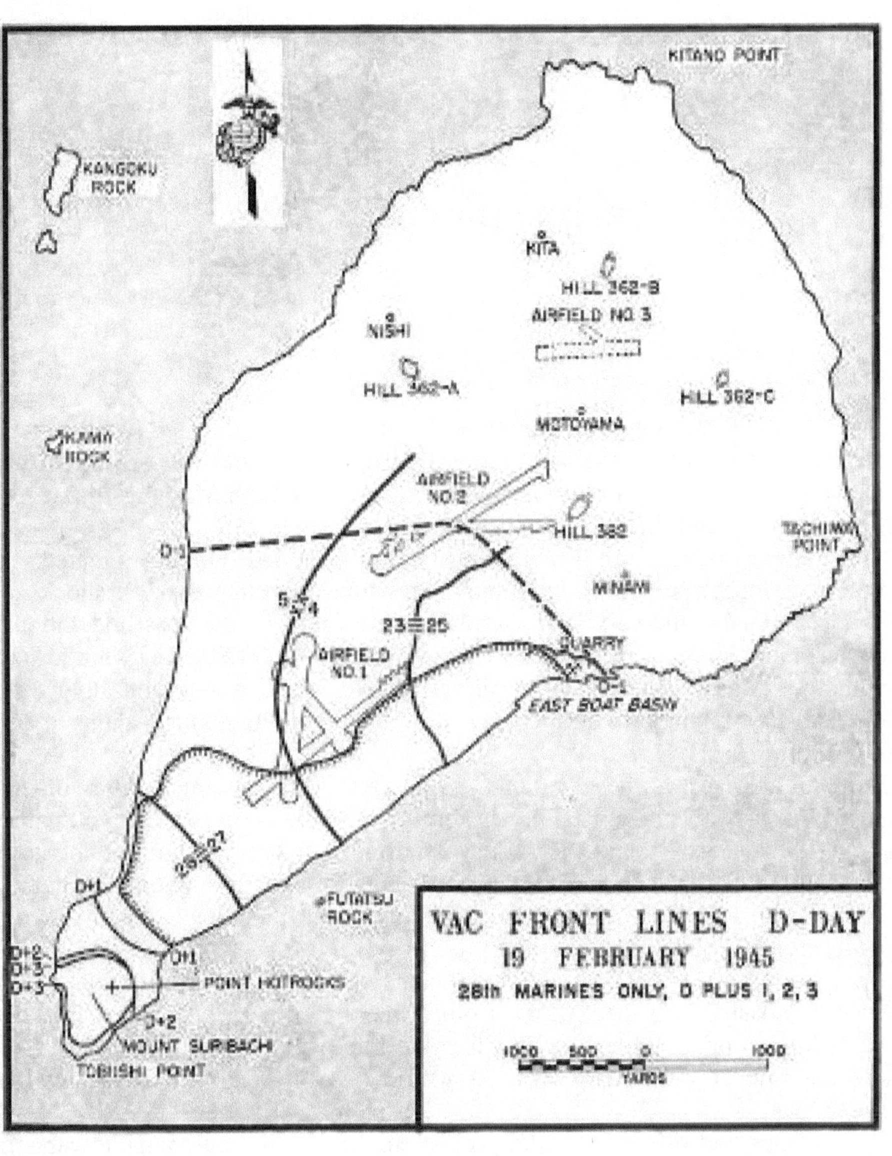

VAC FRONT LINES D-DAY
19 FEBRUARY 1945
28th MARINES ONLY, D PLUS 1, 2, 3

GETTING THE GUNS ASHORE

The greatly filled infantry was bogged down. According to Corporal Ed Hartman, a rifleman in the 4th Marine Division: "the sand was so soft, it was like attempting to run in loose coffee premises." The 28th Marines' first record after obtaining onto land: "resistance modest, terrain horrible."

The moving battery and meticulously implemented landing created the preferred impact: subduing opponent fire while providing enough shock and wonder to enable the very first assault waves to remove the coastline and also advancement internal. In less than fifteen minutes, 6,000 Marines were ashore. Numerous were hindered by raising fire over the terraces and below the highlands, yet hundreds leaped onward and also maintained their assault momentum.

The 28th Marines on the left flank had rehearsed this landing on the volcanic terrain of Hawaii's Big Island. Currently, regardless of boosting casualties amongst firm leaders and the normal landing poor organization, elements of the regiment utilized their campaign to breakthrough throughout the narrow neck of the peninsula. This ended up being much bloodier as enemy strong points along Suribachi's base sprung to life.

Ninety mins after touchdown, components of the 1/28 Marines got to the western coast-- 700 backyards from Green Beach-- Iwo had been cut. According to one Marine: "it was like we removed the serpent's head." This was the inmost infiltration of what would become a expensive as well as bloody day.

The routines had difficulty making clear the black-sand balconies toward the airfield. The surface resembled an open dish in a shooting gallery. Completely view of Suribachi left wing as well as an increasing table to the right. Any type of ideas of this procedure being a cinch rapidly vanished as signed up gatling gun fire whistled throughout the open ground as well as mortar rounds went down along the terraces. Via this hardship, the 27th Marines made good preliminary gains as well as reached the southern and also western sides of the very first landing field by noon.

The 23rd Marines on Yellow Beach took the brunt of the preliminary of opponent integrated arms fire. Troops going across the terrace were challenged by 2 large concrete pillboxes-- still lethal after the bombardment. Getting rid of these settings confirmed expensive in men as well as time as well as. Much more fortified positions increased from the broken ground past. Because of the congestion issues on the beach, demands for storage tank assistance can not be satisfied. Still, the routine clawed its means a number of hundred yards toward the eastern side of the airstrip.

The 25th Marines quickly ran into a "Buzz-Saw" attempting to cross Blue Beach. General Cates was correct in his assessment: "The best flank was a bitch, if there ever was one." The 1/25 Marines scratched, clambered, as well as clawed their method 300 yards ahead under hefty enemy fire in the first half-hour. The 3/25 Marines took the heaviest pounding of the day on the right wing flank while trying to scale the high cliffs bring about the rock quarry.

According to Lieutenant Colonel Justice Chambers leading the 3/25 Marines: "Crossing that second terrace, there was fire from automatic tools originating from all over. I could've stood up a cigarette as well as lit it on right stuff passing. I knew instantly we remained in for one hell of a fight."

However this was only the start. When the touchdown forces attempted to get over the enemy's infantry tools, they were callous an imperceptible mixing happening among the rocks as well as holes in the interior highlands. General Kuribayashi's artillerymans uncovered their big weapons-- huge mortars, hefty artillery, rockets, and also antitank tools held under the tightest technique for simply this precise moment. Kuribayashi had actually waited patiently until the coastlines were blocked with soldiers and product. Gun crews understood the array as well as deflection at each landing coastline by heart: all tools had actually been pre-registered on these targets long ago. At Kuribayashi's signal, numerous tools opened fire. It was quickly after 1030.

This bombardment was as horrifying as well as harmful as any the Marines had ever before experienced. There was no cover. Enemy mortar as well as weapons rounds blanketed every corner of the 3,000-yard-wide coastline. Large quality seaside protection guns and dual-purpose antiaircraft weapons fired flat. This created a harmful scissor of direct fire from the high ground on both flanks.

Militaries stumbled over the terraces to run away the rain of lethal projectiles only to come across machine-gun fire and also minefields. Landing force casualties installed at a stunning rate.

Significant Karch of the 14th Marines expressed a begrudging admiration for the Japanese artillerymans: "it was among the most awful blood-lettings of the war. They rolled weapons barrages backwards and forwards the beach-- I don't see just how any person could've endured such a hefty fire battery. The Japanese were excellent artillerymen-- a person was going to get struck every time they discharged."

At sea, naval shooting support seriously attempted to provide fire against opponent gun settings obliterating from the rock quarry. It took longer to coordinate this fire: the very first opponent batteries erased the whole 3/25 Marines Shore Fire Control Party.

When the Japanese fire reached an upsurge, assault regiments released grim records to the front runner. Within fifteen mins, these messages hummed over the command net:

From 25th Marines 1036: Catching heck from the quarry. Heavy mortar and also machine-gun fire.

From the 23rd Marines 1039: Taking heavy casualties as well as can stagnate ahead. Mortars are killing us.

From the 27th Marines 1042: All units selected by mortars as well as weapons. Heavy casualties. Demand tank support quick to move.

From the 28th Marines 1046: Taking hefty fire and onward movement quit. Artillery as well as machine-gun fire heaviest yet seen.

The touchdown pressure was getting bled but did not panic. The abundance of combat experts throughout the rank-and-file coastline regiments aided the novices concentrate on the objective. Communications were still reliable. Aerial viewers spotted a few of the now exposed weapon placements and also guided efficient naval gunfire. Carrier airplanes screeched in reduced as well as dropped napalm from their stubborn belly tanks. Yet hefty opponent fire continued to take a terrible toll throughout the very first day and night-- but would never once more be as murderous as that initial hour.

Sherman storage tanks played heck getting involved in the activity on D-Day. Later on in the battle, these battle lorries were the most beneficial weapons on the combat zone. This particular day was a nightmare. The assault divisions had embarked lots of containers on board LSMs (Landing Ship Medium), strong craft that could deliver five Shermans each time. It was an obstacle to disembark them on Iwo's high coastlines. The LSMs' demanding supports could not keep in the loose sand

as well as the bow cords split under the stress.

One lead tank delayed on top of the ramp and obstructed the others, leaving the LSM at the mercy of the violent surf. Other storage tanks got or threw tracks slowed down in loose sand. Numerous containers that made it over the terraces were damaged by big horn mines or were disabled by exact 47mm antitank fire from Suribachi. Still, the tanks kept coming. Their flexibility, shield defense, and 75mm guns were a welcome addition to the spread infantry along Iwo's lunar-looking, shell-pocked landscape.

The department commanders committed their books. The 26th Marines were gotten in after midday, General Cates purchased two battalions of the 24th Marines to land at 1400. The 3/24 Marines complied with a number of hrs later on. The book experienced much heavier casualties than the preliminary assault units crossing the coastline, as a result of the punishing adversary barrage from all island points.

Familiar with a possible Japanese counterattack in the night ahead, and regardless of the fire and also complication along the beaches, both departments got their artillery routines onto land. This costly and also irritating procedure took most of the mid-day. The browse and also wind got as the day endured and also caused greater than one low-riding aquatic vehicle to swamp with its valuable 105mm howitzer cargo. Getting the weapons ashore was something; getting them up off the sand was an additional.

The 75mm howitzers did much better than the heavier 105s. Marines can promptly move them up over the balconies-- at considerable risk. However the 105s had a mind of their own in the black sand. The effort to obtain each weapon off the coastline was a legend. Despite unrelenting terrain as well as enemy fire, Marines managed to get the batteries in place and also registered them to provide close-fire support before dark.

Diving surf and also opponent fire transformed the field of battle into utter turmoil. Later that mid-day, Lieutenant Mike Keleher, the squadron surgeon, went onto land to take over the help station. (A sniper had eliminated the previous specialist.) Lieutenant Keleher was an expert of three attack landings. He was stunned by the carnage on Blue Beach: "such a view on the beach. Wrecked watercrafts, bogged down tractors and also jeeps and also containers. Burning cars as well as casualties. Arm or legs of dead Marines were scattered around the beach."

PROWLING WOLVES

An opponent mortar covering took the life of the famous John Basilone. He 'd
led

his gatling gun squad in a take on assault versus the southern portion of the landing strip. All Marines on the island felt this loss. Farther eastern, Colonel Rob Galer (one of the Pacific War's initial fighter aces) endured the afternoon's fight along the coastlines as well as reassembled his scattered radar device in a deep shell-hole near the base of Suribachi.

Later on that mid-day, Colonel Donn Robertson led his Marines onshore to Blue Beach. He was stunned at the strength of fire still routed at the soldiers so late on D-Day: "they awaited us. I saw with satisfaction and wonderment as young Marines landed under attack, took casualties, and stumbled ahead to clear the beach. I asked myself, what impels a young man touchdown on the beach in the face of fire?"

After that it was Robertson's turn. His boat slammed right into the coastline also hard. The ramp wouldn't drop. His Marines needed to roll over the gunwales into the spinning surf and also crawl onto land.

The savage battle to catch the rock quarry cliffs on the appropriate flank raged. The beachhead was subjected to route adversary fire throughout the day. Militaries needed to storm them before any more products or soldiers might be landed. In the end, it was the fighting spirit of Captain James Headley as well as Colonel "Jumping Joe" Chambers who led the survivors of the Marines to the top of the high cliffs.

The battalion paid a high cost for this feat. They 'd lost twenty-two officers and also 5 hundred soldiers by nightfall. Aide division commanders Generals Hart and also Hermle of the 4th and also 5th Marine Division invested a lot of D-Day aboard the control vessels noting both ends of the line a separation -- 4,000 lawns offshore. This was one more lesson in aquatic strategies gained from Tarawa. Having senior police officers near the ship-to-shore motion offered touchdown pressure decision-making from the forward most viewpoint. By dust, General Hermle selected to find ashore. On Tarawa, he 'd spent the night of D-Day out of contact on a fire-swept pierhead. This time around he would be in the battle.

Hermle had the bigger functional photo in mind. He recognized that the corps' leaders persistence on compeling the reserves and artillery units onshore in spite of the carnage to build battle power. Hermle recognized that whatever the night brought, the Allies had extra troops on the island than the Japanese can summon. His existence would assist his division forget the earlier days' calamity as well as concentrate on getting ready for the unpreventable enemy counterattacks.

Opponent mortar as well as weapons fire raked the beachhead. A huge spigot of mortar coverings (Marines called them "flying ashcans") and also rocket-boosted aerial bombs were loud, whistling projectiles that tumbled end over end. Many of them sailed over the island, but those that landed along the coastlines of the southerly runways created dozens of casualties. Couple of Marines can dig a correct foxhole in the sand. It was like attempting to dig a hole in a barrel of wheat. With immediate contact us to the control ship for plasma and also stretchers as well as mortar coverings came repeated sandbag demands.

War fight reporter Lieutenant Cyril Zurlinden (quickly to become a casualty himself) defined his opening night ashore: "On Tarawa, Saipan, and Tinian, I saw Marines injured and eliminated in a stunning fashion. I never ever saw anything like the ghastliness that hung over the Iwo Jima beachhead. It was utter aggravation, misery, and also a constant internal battle to keep at the very least some form of peace of mind.

Accountancy for personnel was a problem under those problems. However assault departments at some point reported a mixed loss of 2,375 males to General Schmidt-- 503 eliminated as well as 1,755 wounded, 18 missing out on, as well as 99 combat disorder. While these data were sobering, Schmidt had gotten 30,000 Marines ashore. A casualty rate of eight percent left the touchdown pressure in much better condition than Saipan or Tarawa's initial day. It was a wonder the casualties hadn't been twice as high. Did Kuribayashi wait as well lengthy to use his large guns?

The opening night in Iwo Jima was an eerie event. Mists of sulfur spiraled from the planet. Marines who were utilized to the tropics now shuddered in the chilly, waiting on Kuribayashi's samurai warriors to find howling down capitals. Militaries learned this Japanese commander was different. There would be no inefficient banzai assault tonight. Instead, small groups of moles, "Prowling Wolves," would certainly penetrate the Marine lines as well as gather intelligence. A barge loaded with the exclusive Japanese Special Landing Forces tried a counter touchdown on the western coastlines-- they passed away to a guy under the alert weapons of the 28th Marines and also supporting LVT crews.

That night was one of continual indirect fire from the Highlands. A high speed round landed directly in a fighting opening occupied by the 1/23 Marines leader Colonel Ralph Hass and instantly killed him. Marines took other light casualties throughout the evening, however at dawn, the veteran landing pressure mixed.

5 infantry programs transferred to the north, while the sixth relied on business handy in the south: Mount Suribachi

SURIBACHI-YAMA

Marines understood this inactive volcano as "Hotrocks.".

The Japanese called it Suribachi-yama. Allied planners recognized their drive north would never ever do well without very first securing that hulking rock dominating the southerly plain. According to one Marine: "Suribachi took on a life of its very own. It supervised us. It towered above us. That hill represented a lot more bad to us than the Japanese.".

Colonel Atsuchi commanded 2,000 enemy soldiers as well as seafarers in the Suribachi fort. The Japanese had actually honeycombed the hill with machine-gun nests, tunnels, as well as observation sites. However Atsuchi had lost a number of his large-caliber weapons from the three-day naval barrage. Atsuchi's command at Suribachi was semiautonomous. General Kuribayashi recognized the intruders would quickly cut communication lines across the island's narrow idea. Kuribayashi really hoped Atsuchi can claim at least 10 days and perhaps even 2 weeks.

Several of the toughest defenses on Suribachi were down along the rubble-scattered base. Below, over seventy camouflaged concrete blockhouses protected the mountain's approaches. An additional fifty blockhouses protruded from the slopes within the first hundred feet of elevation. Then came the caverns, as well as the first of hundreds the Marines would deal with on Iwo Jima.

The 20th Marines took 407 casualties cutting across the neck of the island on D-Day. The complying with day in a chilly rain, they prepared their attack. Colonel Chandler Johnson, regulating the 2/28 Marines, established the early morning's tone as he deployed his worn out troops onward: "it's mosting likely to be a hell of a day in one heck of a location to eliminate this damn war.".

Several 105mm batteries opened overhead. Gun staffs fired from placements dug in the black sand beside the 28th Marine's command article. Troops learned that also their 155mm cannons would hardly shudder the adversary's concrete pillboxes. As the preparatory fire raised, infantry progressed right into heavy mortar and machine-gun fire. Colonel "Harry the Horse" Liversedge requested tanks. The 5th Tank Battalion was having a discouraging morning. Storage tanks frantically looked for a defilade spot to rearm as well as refuel for the assault. In those initial few days on Iwo, there was no such spot. Every time the containers collected to service their vehicles, they were walloped by enemy artillery as well as mortar fire from the whole island. Obtaining the containers serviced to join in on the attack took most of the morning. After getting damaged all day, the tankers would now just renovate, rearm, and also re-equip during the night.

The day's slow-moving start brought about even more obstacles for the 5th Tank Battalion. Enemy antitank artillerymans hid in the patchwork of rocks and knocked senseless the initial coming close to Shermans, debilitating the attack's energy. While the 20th Marines overran forty adversary strongpoints and also got 200 backyards a day, they lost a Marine for every lawn obtained. When a 75mm round caught Colonel Atsuchi poking his head out of a cavern entry-- blowing him apart, the tankers redeemed themselves.

Elsewhere on the early morning of D +1 were dissuading sites of chaos along the coastlines from Kuribayashi's unrelenting artillery batteries and the fierce surf. According to one Marine: "The wreckage was inexpressible. I saw two miles of debris that was so thick there were only a few locations our landing craft could still enter. The wrecked hulls of lots of landing watercrafts testified to the cost we had to pay to place our soldiers onto land. Tanks as well as half-tracks laid there paralyzed from getting slowed down in the coarse sand. LVTs and amphibian tractors were targets of mines and well-aimed shells and were now tumbled on their backs. Cranes were generated to dump cargo and were tilted at outrageous angles. Our excavators were smashed in their very own roads.".

Then bad weather condition embeded in and also complicated the dumping. Strong winds whipped sea swells right into a nasty cut. The surf obtained uglier. These were the problems Colonel Carl Youngdale faced while trying to land the 105mm cannon batteries of his 4/14 Marines. All twelve of these weapons were preloaded in amphibious trucks (DUKWs) one to an automobile. Including in that was the trouble of marginal seaworthiness and polluted fuel. Youngdale seen in shock as 8 amphibious vehicles suffered engine failures, swamped, and also sank with an awful loss of life. Two more amphibious vehicles brought up in the browse area as well as splashed their guns into deep water. Youngdale procured the two remaining weapons onto land as well as right into shooting placement.

General Schmidt committed one battery of the 105mm guns to the narrow beachhead on D +1. These guns got to the coastline intact, but it took hrs to get the aquatic tractors to drag the hefty weapons up over the balconies. The 105's were in location as well as firing prior to dark. The deep bark of the weapons was a welcome sound to the Marines. Concerned about hefty casualties in the first twenty-four hours, General Schmidt dedicated the 21st Marines from the core reserve. But the seas were as well rough. Troops had a harrowing experience trying to get down the cargo nets and also right into the little boats-- violently bobbing alongside the transports. Numerous Marines detected the.

sea. The boating procedure took hrs to complete. Once afloat, troops circled constantly in the small Higgins boats waiting for the call to land. After six hours of bobbing in the water and also terrible motion sickness, the 21st Marines returned to the ships for the evening.

Also the larger touchdown craft, the LSMs and LCTs, had a tough time breaching. Sea supports were required to maintain the craft vertical to the breakers, and also they rarely hung on because soft base. Admiral Hill later composed: "going down that demanding support was like going down a spoon in a bowl of mush.".

Hill added to the growth of aquatic operations in the Pacific War. He as well as his staff created armored bulldozers to land in the attack waves. They experimented with pivoted Marston matting, utilized as a momentary roadway on airfields to get automobiles over soft sand. On the coastline at Iwo, excavators were worth their king's ransom. The Marston matting was just partly effective: the LVTs chewed it up, but all hands can see the true potential. Admiral Hill dealt with the Naval Construction Battalion (Seabees) to bring the supply-laden pontoon barges onto land. But once again, the browse prevailed as well as broached the craft, spilling the freight. Now determined, Hill's beachmasters relied on a continuous use amphibious vehicles and LVTs to keep the battle cargo flowing. As soon as aquatic vehicles broke out of their crippling lots, they were fine.

Amphibian tractors could go across the soft beach without help. They resupplied and also conducted medevac objectives straight along the cutting edge. These automobiles dealt with unskilled staffs in the LSTs who would not lower their bow ramps sufficient to suit the aquatic vehicles as well as tractors approaching night. Many times, automobiles filled with wounded Marines got lost at night or lost ground and also sank. The amphibian tractor squadrons shed over 147 LVTs at Iwo Jima. Unlike Tarawa, where adversary shooting as well as mines represented much less than twenty percent of this total. Thirty- 4 LVTs died from Iwo's squashing surf, and also eighty-eight sank in the deep water.

As soon as onto land and free from the loosened sand along the beaches, half-tracks, containers, as well as armored bulldozers rammed the greatest minefield defenses yet run into in the Pacific. Under Kuribayashi's instructions, enemy designers had actually grown uneven rows of antitank and also horned anti-boat mines along the departures from both beaches.

The opponent accompanied these weapons by rigging huge makeshift explosives from 500-pound airborne bombs, torpedo heads, and deepness charges triggered by a pressure mine. The loosened soil on Iwo had sufficient metallic features to render standard mine detectors incorrect. Marines and also designers were on their hands and also knees before tanks, penetrating for mines with bayonets as well as wood sticks.

While the 28th Marines fought to enclose Suribachi, the coast event and also beachmasters had a hard time to remove the wreck from the coastlines. In the 5th Marine Division area, the fairly fresh troops of the 1/26 and 3/27 Marines got bloodied. They required their means throughout the western runways as well as took hefty casualties from time-fused airbursts and opponent dual-purpose antiaircraft weapons. In the 4th Division area, the 23rd Marines caught and protected the airstrip-- advancing 800 yards with huge casualties.

A few of one of the most vicious battling was along the high ground over the Rock Quarry on the appropriate flank. Right here, the 25th Marines were taken part in the fight of their lives. Rifleman Richard Wheeler located the landscape, and also the ingrained enemy surreal: "there was no cover from opponent fire. Japs were in enhanced concrete pillboxes and also put down interlocking bands of fire that reduced entire firms to pieces. Camouflage concealed all their placements. The high ground on either side was honeycombed with layer after layer of Jap emplacements. They had an excellent observation people. Whenever a Marine made a relocation, those damn Japs surrounded the area with a murderous covering of fire.".

The 2nd day of battle confirmed undesirable on every front for the Marines. When the 1/24 Marines lastly appeared along the high cliffs late in the day, they were rewarded with back-to-back cases of friendly fire. A naval airstrike triggered eleven casualties. Misguided barrages from an unknown gunfire support ship took down one more ninety troops. Absolutely nothing was going. The early morning of D +2 guaranteed more stress. Militaries shuddered in the cool rainfall as well as wind. Since of dangerous undertows and also wicked surf, admiral Hill twice shut the coastline. Throughout one of the poise durations, the 3/21 Marines came onto land, happy to be cost-free of the heaving small boats.

The 20th Marines continued their attack on Suribachi's base. It was a slow, grinding, and bloody fight-- rock by boulder. On the western coastline, the 1/28 Marines made the most of marine as well as field weapons gunfire assistance and also got to the hill's shoulder. Anywhere else, murderous opponent fire.

limited any development to a matter of lawns. Opponent mortar fire from around the volcano drizzled down on the 2/28 Marines, clawing their way along the eastern shore. Rifleman Richard Wheeler remembered: "it was horrible. Worst I can remember us ever taking. Jap mortar men played checkers with us as the squares.".

The Marines used Weasels, convenient tracked vehicles that made their initial field appearance in this battle to hustle onward flamethrower canisters and also evacuate the wounded. That evening the aquatic job pressure experienced the only substantial air assault of the fight. Forty-nine kamikaze pilots from the 22d Mitate Special Attack Unit struck ships on the outer ring of Iwo Jima. In a determined action, working as a start to Okinawa's fiery hell, kamikaze pilots sank the escort provider Bismarck Sea with heavy death. They harmed a number of ships and also knocked the professional Saratoga out of the war. All forty-nine Japanese aircrafts were ruined.

On D +3, it rained also harder. Militaries darted onward under attack, hitting the deck to return fire. They found that the loose volcanic sand, incorporated with rain, obstructed their weapons. The 21st Marines at the lead ran hastily right into a collection of opponent locations at the southeastern end of the Japanese defenses. Militaries fought all the time to scratch and claw and also advance 200 backyards. Casualties were horrific and also out of proportion.

On the appropriate flank, Colonel Chambers rallied the 3/25 Marines via the rough and tough terrain over the Rock Quarry. While Chambers routed the advance of his decimated business, an opponent sniper fired him in the upper body. Chambers dropped hard, believing it was all over: "I faded in and also out. I do not bear in mind excessive about it other than a foamy blood gushing from my mouth. Somebody started kicking the hell out of my feet. It was Captain Headley screaming, 'stand up, you were harmed worse on Tulagi.'".

Captain Headley knew Chamber's drawing chest wound was life- endangering. He attempted to minimize his commander's shock up until he can get him out of the line of fire. Lieutenant Mike Keller, the battalion cosmetic surgeon, crawled forward with one of his corpsmen. They lifted Chambers onto a cot as well as with enemy fire, carried him down the cliffs to the help station, and also at some point onboard an amphibious truck to make the night's last go out to the health center ship. All three squadron commanders on the 25th Marines were currently casualties. Chambers received the medal and made it through of Honor. Captain Headley took command of the shot-up 3/25th Marines for the remainder of.

the battle.

The 20th Marines on D +3 made progression against Suribachi. They got to the shoulder on all factors late in the day. Fight patrols from the 28th Marines linked up at Tobiishi Point: the southern idea of the island. Reconnaissance patrols reported they discovered couple of indicators of life along the hill's top inclines as well as on the north side.

Admiral Spruance authorized Task Force 58 to strike Okinawa and Honshu at dusk. After that, they would certainly go to Ulithi and also get ready for the Ryukyuan project. All 8 Marine Corps boxer armadas left Iwo Jima permanently. Navy pilots flying from the 10 remaining companion carriers grabbed the slack. While there was no doubt of the guts and ability of these pilots, the quality of close air support for the soldiers battling ashore plummeted after the Marine fighter armadas left.

The companion carriers had too many other objectives: fight air patrols, anti-submarine moves, downed pilot searches, and harassing strikes against bordering Chichi Jima. Militaries reported a sluggish reaction time for air support requests, light payloads, and also high shipment elevations. The navy pilots delivered numerous napalm bombs, however numerous fell short to detonate. This wasn't the pilots' mistake. The very early napalm bombs were old wing-tanks full of the mix and also activated by unstable detonators. Marines on the ground were concerned regarding these notoriously unreliable tools being gone down from high altitudes.

On February 23, D +4, the 28th Marines were poised to capture Suribachi. This honor was provided to Lieutenant Harry Schrier as well as Company E, 3rd Platoon. They were ordered to summit, protect the crater, and also increase a 54" x 28" American flag for everyone to see. At 0800, Schrier led his forty-man patrol onward. The routine had actually currently blown up lots of pillboxes with demolitions and flame. They would certainly rooted out snipers and knocked out the mass batteries. The combined arms hammering by planes, naval guns, and also field pieces had actually ultimately taken their toll on the enemy. Any Japanese soldier who popped out of a cavern to resist was cut to shreds. Marines meticulously walked up the high north slope, often resorting to crawling on hands and knees. The Suribachi flag-raising drama has endured for so long since a lot of people observed it. Throughout the island, Marines tracked the development of the small column of soldiers during their climb. Hundreds of field glasses from overseas ships viewed Schrier's Marines climb. When they lastly reached the top, they went away. Those closest to the volcano listened to gunfire. Then at.

1020, there was movement on the summit-- the Stars & Stripes trembled fearlessly in the breeze.

Thanks barked from the southern end of the island. Ships sounded sirens and whistles. Wounded men propped up on their clutters to obtain a peek.

Militaries cried. Navy Secretary Forrestal was thrilled. He relied on General Holland Smith: "elevating that flag implies a Marine Corps for one more 5 hundred years.".

Three hrs later on, an also bigger flag went up. Few recognized that Associated Press photographer Joe Rosenthal had actually simply captured the American battle- fighting spirit on movie. Leatherneck magazine Staff Sergeant Lou Lowery had actually taken an image of the very first flag raising and also right away got involved in a firefight with a handful of infuriated opponent protectors. His photo would come to be a valuable collector's product-- yet it was Rosenthal's that would certainly enchant the totally free world.

Captain Tom Fields of Company D's 1/26 Marines heard his males scream: "Look up there!" and also he kipped down time to see the initial flag rise. His initial thoughts were on the fight still handy, as well as he bore in mind in the minute saying: "Thank God the Japs will not be shooting us down from behind anymore.".

The 28th Marines caught and safeguarded Mount Suribachi in three days at the expense of 900 casualties. Colonel Liversedge reoriented his program for operations to the north. Unidentified to all, the battle of Iwo Jima still had another bloody thirty days prior to it would certainly be over.

THE MEATGRINDER

It wasn't till the nine day of fight that intelligence police officers realized.

General Kuribayashi led the Japanese pressures on Iwo Jima.
The unexpected very early loss of the Suribachi fort was a setback for

Kuribayashi, but he still held a strong setting. He had eight infantry squadrons, 2 weapons and 3 hefty mortar battalions, and a tank routine. Admiral Ichimaru had 5,000 naval infantry as well as artillerymans under his command, however unlike other besieged forts in the Central Pacific-- these 2 Japanese leaders worked well with each other.

Kuribayashi was pleased with the quality of his weapons and design troops. His chief of artillery, Colonel Kaido, regulated from a secure concrete blockhouse in the east-central field of the Motoyama Plateau. A lethal landmark the Marines called "Turkey Knob.".

General Senda was a weapons policeman with battle experience in Manchuria. He regulated the 2d Independent Mixed Brigade, whose main systems would certainly be secured right into a 25-day death resist the 4th Marine Division. The 204th Naval Construction Battalion had actually developed some of the most powerful protection systems on the island in his sector. One cavern had an 800-foot-long tunnel with fourteen different exits. It was only one of the hundreds protected to the death.

Well-armed and also certain adversary troops waited for the advance of the V Amphibious Corps. Kuribayashi bought periodic company-sized assaults to regain lost surface or disrupt enemy assault preparations-- but these were not sacrificial or suicidal. These generally were come before by stinging mortar and also artillery fires and also targeted at gaining restricted objectives. General Kuribayashi's iron will maintained his troops from massive, futile banzai assaults till the last few days.

An exception was on the evening of March 8. General Senda, annoyed at the noose the 4th Division were using, bought 800 of his making it through troops right into a vicious counterattack. Finally, the Marines had targets exposed. The self-destructive Japanese enemies were cut to pieces with machine-gun and little arms fire.

For the initial week of the drive north, the Japanese on Iwo had the attacking Marines outgunned. The opponent's 120mm mortars and 150mm guns were superior to the majority of the tools of the landing force. Militaries discovered the enemy's straight fire tools fatal. Especially the dual-purpose antiaircraft weapons and also the 47mm tank guns, buried up to their turrets. Retired General Donn Robertson claimed: "the Japs could snipe with those huge weapons. They likewise had the advantage of understanding the ground.".

The majority of the casualties in the first 3 weeks of battle were from high nitroglycerins: rocket bombs, explosives, mines, artillery, and also great mortars. Robert Sherrod (Time reporter) created that the dead on Iwo Jima, both Japanese as well as Marine, had one point alike: "they all passed away with the greatest feasible violence. Nowhere in the Pacific War had I seen such badly mangled bodies. Lots of guys were cut squarely in half.".

The close fight was vicious. An additional consistent stress and anxiety for Marines was no protected back area to place wounded soldiers. Kuribayashi's gunners hammered the landing strips as well as beaches. Enormous spigot mortar coverings and rocket bombs tumbled from the sky. Japanese defenders were drawn to softer targets in the back. Anti-personnel mines and also booby-traps were anywhere as well as widespread for the first time in the Pacific.

Exhausted Marines stumbled out of the front line, seeking nothing more than a helmet packed with water to wash in and also a deep hole to sleep in. Rather, Marines spent their uncommon remainder repairing tools, dodging incoming rounds, humping ammo, or having to fend off an additional nighttime adversary probe.

General Schmidt intended to attack the northern Japanese positions with three departments informed. The 5th on the left, the 3rd in the facility, and also the 4th on the right. This north drive would embark on D +5: the day after protecting Mount Suribachi. Primary fires along the high ground north of the second airfield would last for an hour. Then three regimental battle groups would certainly progress abreast: 26th Marines left wing, 24th on the right, and the 21st in the facility. For this assault, Schmidt combined all three departments' Sherman containers into one armor task pressure-- regulated by Colonel "Rip" Collins. This would certainly be the largest concentration of Marine tanks in the Pacific War: an armored regiment.

Militaries recognized they were trying to require a passage via Kuribayashi's primary protective belt. The attack weakened into numerous hopeless small unit activities along the front. While the 26th Marines (with the assistance of tanks) acquired the most lawns, it was still family member. Landing field runways were dangerous murder areas. Mines as well as high-velocity direct fire ruined Sherman tanks all along the front. On the appropriate flank, Colonel Alexander Vandegrift (child of Marine Commandant Alexander Vandegrift) was wounded.

Throughout the combating on D +5, General Schmidt relocated his command post onshore from the aquatic force front runner Auburn. Schmidt now had 8 whole infantry regiments devoted to the fight. General Holland Smith still had the 3rd Marines and also expeditionary troops aside. Schmidt made his initial of several demands to Smith to release that skilled outfit. The V Amphibious Corps had already taken 6,845 casualties.

On February 25, D +6, adversary resistance escalated. Tiny Marine units accompanied by storage tanks made progress along the path. Each Marine was under the perception he was alone in the center of a gigantic bowling lane. Usually, holding newly gotten settings across the path verified more deadly than recording them. Resupplying the troops ended up being virtually impossible. Precious Sherman tanks were obtaining ruined at a startling price.

General Schmidt obtained two squadrons of 105mm howitzers onto land under the command of Colonel John Letcher. Well-directed fire from these heavy area pieces eased a few of the stress on the attacking Marines. While fire from cruisers and also destroyers was marginally efficient, air assistance was an overall disappointment. The 3rd Marine Division later on whined that the Navy's assignment of eight fighters as well as 8 bombing planes on station was entirely poor.

At twelve noon, General Cates sent out a message to Schmidt asking for the strategic Air Force in the Marianas right away change Navy air assistance. Colonel McGee, air commander on Iwo, took heat from the irritated department leaders. He later created: "those little spit set Navy boxers up there were attempting to assist yet were never adequate and were never where they needed to be."

In fairness, it's open to question if any service could have given adequate air support within the opening days of the northern drive. The air liaison celebrations within each regiment played hell attempting to determine and also note targets. The adversary maintained a skillful camouflage. Japanese frontline units were often eyeball to eyeball with Marines, and the air assistance demand net was typically overloaded.

Navy squadrons flying from the decks of companion providers eventually enhanced by including larger bombs and also enhancing their reaction times. A week later on, General Cates ranked his air assistance as acceptable. Yet the battle of Iwo Jima would certainly remain to frustrate Allied forces; the Japanese never ever set up legit targets outdoors. Captain Fields of the 26th Marines composed after the war: "the Japs weren't on Iwo Jima. They remained in Iwo Jima."

Richard Wheeler, that survived Iwo Jima with the 28th Marines, created two books concerning the fight. "This was one of the strangest battlegrounds in background. One side dealt with completely over ground, and the various other run within it. Throughout the fight, American airborne viewers marveled that side of the area had hundreds of numbers circling or in foxholes while the other side was deserted. The strangest of all was that the 2 candidates sometimes made army activities all at once in the very same region with one handling on the surface area and the other making use of passages below."

As the Marines dealt with like hell to record the 2nd airfield from the Japanese, the terrain features climbing to the north captured their attention. While there were 3 hills called 362 on the island, Marines had various nicknames for them: "Amphitheater" and "Turkey Knob." Yet the bristling complicated of hillsides and terrain would be forever referred to as "The Meatgrinder."

The 5th Marine Division made their stimulates as well as lost many of their valuable veteran leaders combating on "The Gorge" and also attacking Nishi Ridge (Hills 362-An and B).

The 3rd Marine Division concentrated their attack north of the 2nd airfield and after that onto the greatly fortified Hill 362-C past the airstrip. Finally, they assaulted the moonscape jungle of stone, quickly to be called "Cushman's pocket."

Colonel Robert Cushman commanded the 2/9 Marines on Iwo. Cushman and also his Marines were professionals of hefty battling on Guam yet were stunned by their first sight of the combat zone. Burned out and smoldering Sherman containers populated airstrips. Casualties streamed to the back. The terrific and horrific resemble of machine-gun fire was anywhere. Cushman installed his soldiers on the surviving tanks and grumbled throughout the field. They met the same reverse- slope defenses that dogged the 21st Marines. However after three days of savage battling, Cushman's Marines secured the two Hills north of the second landing strip, Peter as well as 199-Oboe.

General Schmidt made the 3rd Division assault in the facility of his main initiative. He offered the 3rd priority fire assistance from the corps artillery. He directed the other 2 departments to allot half of their regimental fire assistance to the center. The other commanders were not pleased. Neither the 4th Marine Division, who took heavy casualties in the Amphitheater, nor the 5th Division, who had a hard time to seize Nishi Ridge, wished to weaken their natural fire support.

General Graves Erskine argued the main effort needs to get the key fire. Schmidt never solved this problem. His corps artillery was far too late, and also he needed two times as several squadrons as well as larger guns: the 8-inch howitzers, which the Marines had not yet fielded. Schmidt had plenty of marine shooting assistance offered and also utilized it generously. Unless targets were in gorges dealing with the sea-- he lost the advantage of observed straight fire.

General Schmidt's fire assistance problems were relieved on February 26. Two Marine observation aircrafts flew in from the carrier Wake Island and were the initial airplanes to land on Iwo's recently recaptured, fire brushed up major airstrip.

These were single-engine observation airplanes (Grasshoppers). They were adhered to the following day by similar airplanes from VMO-5. The pilots of these breakable aircrafts had already had an exciting time in the waters off Iwo. Numerous were released from the experimental catapult on LST-776: "like a peanut from a slingshot."

All fourteen of these monitoring aircrafts took hefty enemy fire airborne as well as while serviced on the airstrips. These 2 squadrons flew 612 objectives supporting all three departments. Few units added as much to the ultimate reductions of Kuribayashi's homicidal weapons fire. The simple presence of the tiny aircrafts overhead caused Japanese gunners to stop fire as well as button-up against the inescapable counter-battery fire quickly to follow. Grasshopper pilots would fly predawn or dirt goals to expand a protective umbrella over the soldiers. Due to the fact that of Iwo's unlit areas as well as snipers concealed in the hills, this was risky flying.

When the 4th Marine Division finally safeguarded Hill 382 at the acme north of Suribachi, they still suffered heavy casualties relocating via the Amphitheater against Turkey handle. The 5th Marine Division took Nishi Ridge as well as bloodied themselves on Hill 362-A's elaborate defenses. Colonel Tom Wornham, CO, 27th Marines: "they had interlacing fields of fire the similarity which I would certainly never ever seen before."

General Cates redeployed the 28th Marines into the fight. On March 2, an opponent gunner fired a high-velocity shell that eliminated Colonel Chandler Johnson one week after his glorious seizure of the Suribachi Summit. The 28th Marines caught Hill 362-A-- at the price of 200 casualties.

The same day, Colonel Lowell English, CARBON MONOXIDE 2/21 Marines, took a bullet in his knee. Colonel English was upset that his squadron was not rotating to the rear: "We were as well as took heavy casualties messed up. I had less than 300 Marines left of the 1,200 I came onto land with." Colonel English received orders to turn his Marines around as well as plug a gap in the cutting edge. "It was an impossible order. I could not move that chaotic battalion a mile back to the north in thirty minutes."

General Erskine did not want reasons: "tell that God-damned English he 'd much better be there."

Colonel English replied: "you tell that boy of a bitch I will certainly exist, and I was, however my men were still half a mile behind me, and also I obtained an opening in my knee!"

The 26th Marines combated their bloodiest and also most effective strike of the fight on the left flank-- finally safeguarding Hill 362-B. This all-day battle expense 500 Marine casualties and also created five Medals of Honor. For Captain Frank Caldwell of Company F, 1/26 Marines, it was the most awful day of his life. His company took forty-nine casualties on that hill-- in addition to the initial sergeant and also all the original squad commanders.

The very first nine days of the V Amphibious Corps' northern drive generated an internet gain of just 4,000 lawns at a dreadful expense of 7,000 Marine casualties. Several of these battle royals in The Meatgrinder would've deserved a separate publication. The battling was among the most bloody and brutal in the Marine Corps' history.

On D +13, March 4, came the transforming point. After alarming as well as shocking losses, Marines had torn with a substantial chunk of General Kuribayashi's key defenses. Compeling the enemy commander to change his command article to a north cavern. On this mid-day, the very first paralyzed B-29 landed. In regards to Allied morale, it couldn't have come at a much better time. General Schmidt got a standdown on March 5 to make it possible for the exhausted assault pressures a short remainder and also the possibility to absorb substitutes.

The concern of replacement soldiers throughout this fight is questionable-- even seventy-seven years later. General Schmidt had actually experienced losses coming close to the equivalent of a whole division (6,561 Marines). Schmidt prompted Holland Smith to release the 3rd Marines. While each department had actually been designated several thousand Marine substitutes, Schmidt desired the cohesion and also combat experience of Colonel Jim Stewart's regimental battle group. Holland Smith suggested the substitutes would be enough and believed that each replacement Marine in these hybrid devices had received enough infantry training to allow his immediate project to the frontline outfits.

The next challenge was distributing the replacements in tiny approximate numbers-- not teamed systems-- to connect the open openings in the attack squadrons. These new men were anticipated to change the vital professionals of the Pacific War. These substitute Marines were not just brand-new to battle however additionally per other-- an array of unfamiliar people that did not have the lifesaving bonds of unit honesty.

One frustrated Marine police officer said: "they obtain eliminated the day they go into fight." Losses among the substitute Marines within the first forty-eight hrs of combat were shocking. Those that endured and also found out the ropes developed a bond with the professionals as well as contributed substantially to the fight's success. Department commanders criticized the profligacy of this policy and advised for substitutes from the professional squadrons of the 3rd Marines.

General Erskine later on wrote: "I asked Kelly Turner and also Holland Smith to give us the 3rd. They stated, 'you got enough Marines on the island now. There are too damn many below currently.' I said, 'this is an easy remedy. Several of these Marines are tired and also worn out, so take them out and also bring in the goddamn 3rd Marines.' They said, 'maintain your mouth shut. We made our choice.' Which was that."

The majority of making it through policemans agreed that the choice not to use the expert 3rd Marines at Iwo was inefficient and also ill-advised. Holland Smith never fluctuated: "adequate soldiers were on Iwo Jima for the capture of the island. Two regiments sufficed to cover the frontal attack assigned to General Erskine."

On D +14, March 5, General Holland Smith ordered the 3rd Marines to sail back to Guam.

While Holland Smith might have understood the general data of the battle losses endured by the touchdown pressure then-- he did not completely value the significant attrition of knowledgeable junior police officers as well as senior noncoms taking their area each day. The day after the 3rd Marines cruised for Guam, the 2/23 Marines' E Company endured the loss of their 7th company leader given that the start of the battle.

Colonel Cushman's experiences with the 2/9 Marines were common: "casualties were ruthless. By the time Iwo mored than, we would certainly gone through two full collections of lieutenants and also platoon leaders. Afterwards, we had forward artillery viewers commanding companies and also sergeants leading half strength platoons. It was that negative."

Colonel English created: "After twelve days, we 'd lost every business commander. I had one company director left. I 'd shed all 3 of my rifle company leaders eliminated by the same damn covering."

Several infantry systems and also squads disappeared. Depleted firms were merged to create half-strength clothing.

NORTHERN ALLIED DRIVE

The Allied drive continued north after the March 5 standdown. It did not obtain any type of easier. The Japanese had changed methods: fewer large weapons and also rockets and also much less observed fire from the highlands. Currently, the terrain had degraded

into narrow twisted canyons, wrapped up in sulfur mists-- eliminating areas.

Allied casualties mounted. Gunshot wounds now exceeded the high eruptive shrapnel hits. A misconception amongst Marine systems was that the Japanese were bad as well as myopic marksmen. In close quarters battling in north Iwo, Japanese riflemen rejected hundreds of advancing Marines in the head or upper body with well-aimed fire. Captain Caldwell of the 1/26 Marines claimed: "Poor marksmen? All the Japs we faced were professional shooters."

Supporting arms coordination came to be extra effective during the fight. Colonel "Buzz" Letcher established the very first SACC (Supporting Arms Coordination Center), where senior weapons, naval shooting, as well as air support agents merged their resources as well as abilities. While Letcher did not have the workforce and communications tools to run a permanent SACC, his initiatives significantly advanced this difficult art.

Colonel McGee's Landing Force Air Support Control Unit operated in consistency with the new SACC. Still, friendly fire events happened. Maybe pleasant fire was unavoidable on that particular jampacked island, but favorable control at the highest degree did a lot to decrease the frequency of these crashes.

The absence of initial marine barrage on Iwo outraged Marines. While all hands valued the receptive assistance received from D-Day forward, the lack of first fire was criticized for the terrible Marine casualties. The gunfire ships stood in close-- less than a mile offshore-- and also hammered the flanks and cutting edges. Several ships took hits from the covert enemy coastal defense batteries. There were no risk-free zones in or around Iwo Jima.

2 qualities of naval gunfire on Iwo were notable: The level ships offered illuminating rounds over the battleground, particularly throughout the early days prior to the touchdown force artillery can presume the bulk of these missions. Secondly was the degree helpful supplied by the smaller sized gunships, regularly modified with 4.2-inch mortars, 20mm weapons, or rockets. These "little boys" were crucial along the northwestern coast as they worked in lockstep with the 5th Marine Division advancing toward The Gorge.

While the Marines consisted of a lot of the landing pressure on Iwo, they still received support from the army. 2 of the four amphibious vehicle firms on D-Day were military systems. The 138th Antiaircraft Artillery Group placed their 90mm batteries around the newly caught landing strips. General Jim Chaney (later to come to be Iwo's island commander) arrived at D +8 with components of the Army's 145th Infantry.

Army devices flew right into Iwo on March 6 (D +15). The 15th Fighter Group showed up to companion B-29s over Tokyo. This group was a seasoned attire that consisted of the well-known 47th Fighter Squadron as well as their P-51 Mustangs. While the army pilots had little to no experience in straight air assistance of ground soldiers, Colonel McGee was thrilled with their "excited beaver attitude" and determination to learn.

McGee appreciated the reality the Mustangs could provide thousand-pound bombs. He had the Army pilots educated on how to strike assigned targets on close-by islands. In three days, they were ready for duty on Iwo. McGee instructed the Mustang pilots to equip their bombs with twelve-second hold-up integrates and strike alongside the front lines coming close to from a 45 ° angle.

These tactics usually produced stunning results-- especially along the west coast-- where the thousand-pound bombs blew sides of entire cliffs off into the ocean. This revealed opponent caverns and passages to direct marine gunfire from the sea. According to McGee: "those Air Force children did a lot of good."

The field clinical assistance offered to the assaulting Marines was a major contributor to success on Iwo. Incorporating pastors, doctors, as well as corpsmen within the FMF (Fleet Marine Force) paid valuable rewards. Most times, corpsmen were as challenging and fight savvy as the Marines because company. Damaged Marines understood their corpsman would certainly move paradise as well as earth to reach them, bind their wounds, and also start the long evacuation process.

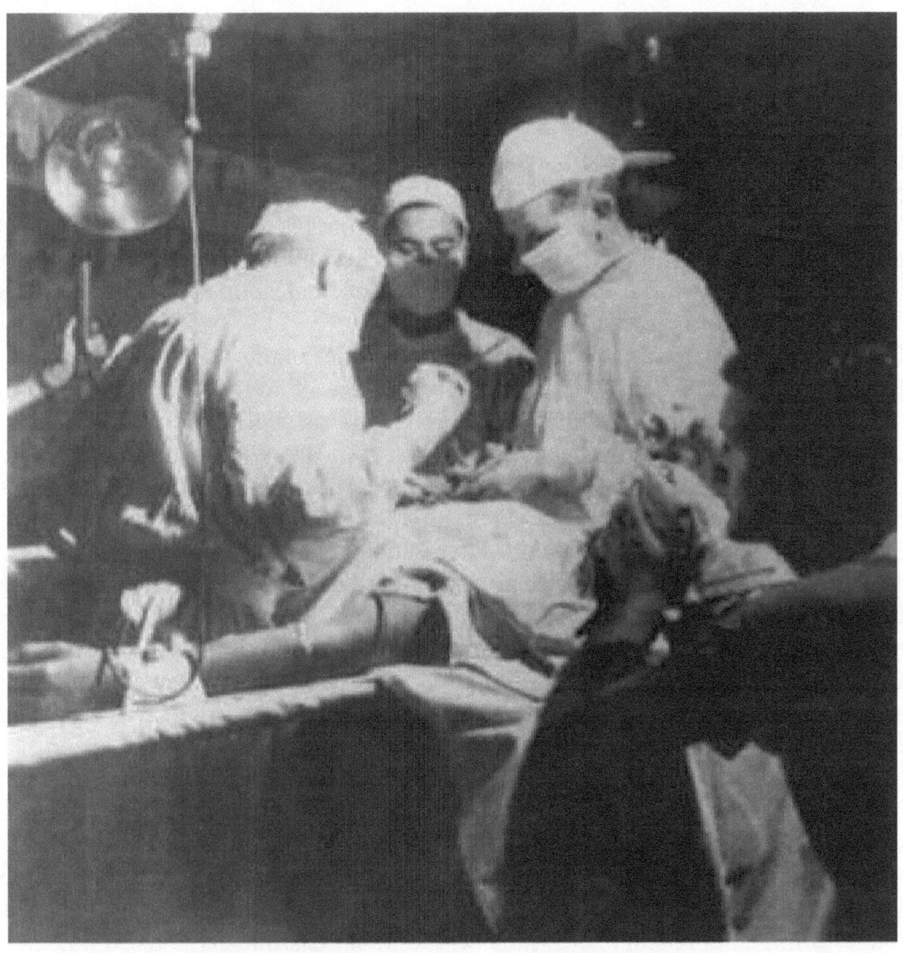

Marines on Iwo Jima echoed the views of Staff Sergeant Al Thomas: "we had impressive corpsmen. They were our household." The deluxe of having premium clinical assistance so near to the front took an awful toll. Eight hundred twenty-seven corpsmen and also twenty-three medical professionals were wounded or eliminated on Iwo Jima-- a casualty rate two times as high as Saipan.

Fight medical support was thoughtfully ready as well as provided on Iwo. Past the crude help terminals and towards the rear, the Army as well as Navy field

hospitals developed. Injured Marines would certainly obtain therapy in an area medical facility, after that recover in a bunker prior to returning to the lines to typically obtain their third or 2nd wound. The even more seriously injured were left by air to Guam or to among the a number of fully-staffed healthcare facility ships running around the clock. Within the first month of fighting on Iwo, 13,747 Marines and corpsmen casualties were evacuated by hospital ship and also an additional 2,489 by airlift.

When a Marine was injured, the initial few minutes were the most harmful after dropping. Adversary snipers had no hesitations about selecting off corpsmen, clutter staffs, and even the wounded male himself as his buddies tried to slide him out of the fire.

Corporal Ed Canter was a rocket vehicle crew chief in the 4th Marine Division. Rocket vehicles constantly drew an angry barrage of counter-battery fire from the enemy. A Japanese sniper shot Canter via the belly. Corporal Canter's comrades recognized they needed to obtain him away from that launch site quick. As a nearby movie crew videotaped the dramatization, 4 Marines brought Canter down a mud-covered hillside. They heard the scream of an incoming shell as well as dumped Canter while they hid.

The explosion killed the movie team and injured each of the Marines, including Canter once more. The movie footage survived and also showed up in US newsreels-- before coming to be a component of the movie Sands of Iwo Jima. Corporal Canter was and also endured left to a health center ship and afterwards to different health centers in Guam and Hawaii before returning to the United States. His war was over.

The shore event workers and also beachmasters done amazing feats of logistics to maintain the advancing departments geared up and armed. The logistical administration as well as sheer gruelling work needed to keep such a high volume of products and also tools conforming these harmful beaches was tough to imagine. A single coastline on the west coastline came to be practical on D.

+11, but by that time, the majority of the touchdown force materials were currently ashore. The following day after the basic dumping was completed, the at risk aquatic ships were launched from their tether to the beachhead. Quickly after, well-aimed enemy fire detonated the 5th Marine Division's whole ammo dump. Ammo resupply became crucial. After that, the ammo ship.

Columbia Victory came under straight opponent fire as she approached the western coastlines to unload. Waiting Marines held their breath as the

Columbia Victory was almost destroyed. She directly got away, however the potential for calamity still loomed.

An entire brigade of the 62nd Naval Construction Battalion (Seabees) expanded and fixed the captured paths. Marines going back to the coastlines from the northern highlands might scarcely acknowledge the place they 'd initially seen on D-Day. There were currently over 80,000 Allied soldiers on the tiny island, as well as the Seabees had actually bulldozed a two-lane roadway to the top of Mount Suribachi.

Communications had actually enhanced drastically on Iwo contrasted to previous amphibious projects. Handsets and radios were currently water resistant and had a lot more regularities. Ahead observer teams used the knapsack SCR- 610, while business and also platoons preferred the walkie-talkie style SCR-300 and even lighter portables, the "Spam Can" SCR-536.

Colonel Jim Berkeley, XO of the 27th Marines said: "On Iwo, we had near-perfect interactions. It was all any leader can ask for." Militaries strung telephone lines in between assistance units as well as 4 command messages as the battle raved, boosting the wire along upright blog posts to avoid damage by tracked cars.

Opponent counterintelligence anticipated to have an easy day splicing into allied phone lines, yet Marines baffled them with Navajo code talkers. Each division employed twenty-four qualified Navajos. The 5th Marine Division's command article had 6 recognized Navajo networks on the island. No person throughout the battle could ever fracture the Navajo code.

Black American soldiers played a major role in the capture of Iwo. Black soldiers drove military aquatic trucks as well as were active throughout the landing. Black Marines of the 8th Ammunition Company and also the 36th Depot Company came down on D-Day and also served as longshoremen on those chaotic, bloody beaches. The on-island Black Marines collaborated with the Shore Party and helped to endure the energy of the Allied north drive. When the Japanese counterattacked penetrated these beach areas, Black Marines dropped their freight, unslung their carbines, as well as involved the opponent with well-disciplined fire.

Colonel Leland Swindler commanded the V Amphibious Corps Shore Party: "the whole body of Black Marines under my command conducted themselves with marked coolness as well as guts and brought upon even more casualties.

on the adversary than they maintained.".

Information coverage of the Iwo Jima battle was extensive. Lots of fight contributors were installed with the touchdown pressure throughout the fight.

Marine Sergeant "Dick" Dashiell was a writer for the Associated Press as well as designated to the 3rd Marine Division. Although often frightened and filled with scary, Dashiell endured and also created eighty-one frontline stories as well as pounded out press release on his mobile typewriter beside his foxhole. Dashiell's eye for detail constantly caught the interest of the reader: "All is bitter. Frontal assault constantly uphill. A continuous wind loaded the air with a great volcanic grit." He defined just how Marines needed to stop and also clean up the grit from their tools-- and just how naked that made most Marines really feel.

Occasionally, warm food was supplied to the tired Marines on the cutting edge. The distribution of milk as well as fruit from close-by ships boosted spirits.

Did enjoying the crippled B-29s zoom in for an emergency landing. Sergeant "Doc" Lindsey was a squad leader in Company G, 2/25 Marines. He specified: "It was excellent to see them land. You understood they 'd simply originate from striking Tokyo.".

DEFIANT TO THE END

General Erskine caught pneumonia yet rejected to leave. His Chief of Staff, Colonel Robert Hogaboom, kept the battle moving behind the scenes. The department proceeded its breakthrough, and also when Erskine recuperated-- Hogaboom changed accordingly. Both were an efficient team.

Erskine had long wanted to perform a battalion-size evening operation. It bothered him that throughout the battle, the Allies had generated the evening to the Japanese. When Hill 362-C remained to obstruct his development, Erskine got a predawn attack without the features of preparatory fire, which constantly identified the time and place of strike.

The honor of leading this uncommon strike was propounded Colonel "Bing" Boehm, CO, 3/9 Marines. But this battalion was new to the field as well as received their attack order too late to examine efficiently. Lacking of development alignment, the battalion went across the line of separation quietly at 0500 as well as advanced towards Hill 362-C. The system attained total shock. Before the sleepy Japanese knew it, the Marines swept throughout 500 lawns of broken ground and also baked adversary outposts and also strengths with weapons.

When daytime disclosed that Boehm's squadron had captured the wrong hillside (Hill 362-C was still 250 yards distant), his squadron was surrounded by a sea of angry and wide-awake as well as counterattacking adversary infantry. Boehm redeployed his squadron as well as attacked toward the initial hillside. This was harsh going as well as took most of the day, but before dark, the 3/9 Marines safeguarded Hill 362-C-- a primary Japanese defensive support.

The Allied settings grew stronger after General Senda's counterattack versus the 4th Marine Division. On D +18, a patrol from the 3rd Marine Division got to the northeast coast. The squad leader filled his canteen with deep sea and also sent it to General Schmidt marked: "For Inspection, Not Consumption."

Schmidt welcomed the significance. The next day, the 4th Marine Division lastly secured Turkey Knob and also advanced towards The Amphitheater on the eastern shore. While completion was in sight, the intensity of the Japanese resistance did not discolor. In the 5th Division's western area, the 2/26 reported a casualty rate of seventy percent. General Keller Rockey reported his Marines were: "in a state of extreme exhaustion as well as fatigue."

Division leaders sought to eliminate their shot-up males. General Cates created a provisionary squadron in the 4th Marine Division under Colonel Melvin Krulewitch. He was gotten to assault bypassed opponent settings. While the term "mopping up" was utilized, it was taken into consideration inaccurate by numerous Allied soldiers. Plenty of pockets of Japanese held up-- bold and well-armed to the end. Rooting them out was never ever very easy. Marines utilized leaders, electric motor transportation systems, as well as amtracs, as light infantry devices to strengthen frontline squadrons and conduct battle patrols.

In the severe back on Iwo Jima, the males had ended up being overconfident.

Films were revealed every evening and also ice cream can be found on the coastline. Men swam in the browse and also slept in tents in a false as well as harmful feeling of security.

To the north, Colonel Cushman's 2/9 Marines were taken part in busted terrain eastern of the airfield. Militaries eventually enclosed the adversary's placement, however the fight of "Cushman's Pocket," raged on. Cushman's squadron leader reported the activity: "The Jap setting is a puzzle of pillboxes, caverns, emplaced tanks, trenches, as well as stonewalls. We beat versus them for 8 constant days making use of every assistance weapon. Our core purpose in the field still stays. Our battalion is tired, as well as a lot of our leaders are gone. Our squadron currently numbers 387 with 350 replacements."

Cushman's 2/9 was eventually alleviated by elements of the 9th as well as 21st Marines (similarly worn down) and also had equally as challenging of a time. General Erskine had no reserves. He ordered Cushman back right into the pocket, and by March 16, (D +25) adversary resistance in the thicket of jumbled rocks ended.

The 4th Marine Division put over capitals in the east and safeguarded the coastal roadway by blowing up the last Japanese strengths from the back. Ninety percent of Iwo Jima was in Allied hands. Radio Tokyo revealed the autumn of Iwo Jima as: "the most unfortunate point in the entire battle circumstance."

General Holland Smith took the opportunity to proclaim success as well as perform a flag-raising ceremony. Following that, the old warhorse departed together with Admiral Kelly Turner. Currently, General Schmidt and also Admiral Hill ultimately had the project to themselves. Survivors of the 4th Marine Division began backloading on board ship-- their battle ultimately over.

The eliminating continued in the north. The 5th Marine Division got in The Gorge, an 800-yard pocket of busted nation the soldiers called "Death Valley." General Kuribayashi would make his last stand below in a command facility in a deep cave. Battling through this nasty moonscape was a fitting end to the fight-- 9 days of cave-by-cave attacks with demolitions and flamethrowers. Marine battle engineers utilized 9,000 tons of explosives to detonate one massive fortification. Progress was sluggish and also bloody. General Rockey's depleted and also drained regiments shed one man for every 2 yards got. General Schmidt deployed the 3rd Division against Kitano Point in the 5th Division zone to reduce the pressure.

Colonel Hartnoll Withers led the last attack with the 21st Marines against the severe northern pointer of the island. General Erskine's pneumonia be damned. He went along to look over Withers' shoulder. The 21st Marines felt completion was near. Their momentum was alluring. In a few hours of sharp battling, they cleaned out the last of the resistance. Erskine signaled Schmidt: "Kitano Point Taken."

Allied forces tried to persuade Kuribayashi to surrender during these last days. They broadcasted allures in Japanese as well as sent him personal messages, commending his valor, as well as urging his teamwork. General Kuribayashi was a samurai to the end. In his last message to Tokyo: "We have not consumed or consumed for 5 days, but our battling spirit is still running high. We will battle to the end for our Emperor."

Imperial Headquarters tried to share the good news that the emperor had authorized his promotion to full basic. There was no response from Iwo Jima. It would be a posthumous promo. Questionable Japanese proof disclosed that he dedicated Seppuku on the evening of March 25.

The 5th Marine Division clawed their method forward in The Gorge. The average squadron that landed with thirty-six officers and 885 males on D-Day now just had sixteen police officers and 300 males. This included the thousands of substitutes funneled in through the battle. Remnants of the 1/26 and also 1/28 Marines squeezed the opponent right into a final pocket as well as destroyed them.

On the night of March 25 (D +34), the fight for Iwo Jima mored than. The island became strangely silent. Far less illumination shells flickered a false light on the shadowy numbers relocating south towards the landing strip. General Schmidt got the bright side that the 5th Marine Division had actually offed the last adversary cave. As the corps commander prepared to declare the end of organized resistance on Iwo Jima-- a well-organized adversary pressure emerged from the northern caves and snuck down the size of the island.

This last convulsion of Japanese resistance showed the enemy's tactical technique. A 300-man Japanese pressure took all evening to relocate into position around the island's vulnerable rear location. Newly arrived army pilots from the VII Fighter Command were shocked in their camping tents. The opponent force attacked the resting pilots with grenades, swords, and automatic rifles. The battling was as vicious and also bloody as any on Iwo Jima.

Male from the 5th Pioneer Battalion as well as surviving pilots formed an altercation line as well as introduced a counterattack. Seabees and also redeploying 28th Marines joined the fight. There were few suicides among the Japanese. The majority of passed away in battle. Grateful to strike one last strike for their emperor. Dawn uncovered the carnage-- 300 dead enemy and over a hundred slaughtered pilots, Seabees, as well as leaders along with another 200 wounded. It was a grotesque closing phase to 5 savage weeks of murder as well as carnage.

LEGACY OF IWO JIMA

In thirty-six days of battle, the V Amphibious Corps killed nearly 22,000 Japanese sailors and soldiers. This was attained at an astonishing price. Marine

attack units (together with organic Navy personnel) experienced 24,053 casualties

-- 6,140 eliminated-- the highest single action losses in Marine Corps history. Statistically, for every three Marines who landed on Iwo Jima, one ended up being a casualty.

According to armed forces chronicler Norman Cooper: "Seven hundred Americans provided their lives for each square mile. For every plot of ground the size of a football field, an average of one American and also 5 Japanese were eliminated, and five Americans wounded."

Attack devices birthed the impact of these casualties. Captain Bill Ketcham's Company I, 3/24 Marines, arrived on D-Day with 133 Marines as well as three rifle armies. When his company re-embarked on D +35, just 9 of these guys continued to be.

Captain Frank Caldwell reported a loss of 220 men from Company F, 1/26 Marines. By the end, a personal extraordinary commanded a platoon in Captain Caldwell's merged 1st and 2nd Platoons.

Captain Tom Fields relinquished command of Company D on the 8th day to replace his squadron's executive officer. When he rejoined his business at the end of the fight, Fields was upset to discover just seventeen of the initial 250 Marines still alive.

Business B of the 1/28 Marines went through 9 company commanders in the fight. Twelve various Marines served as army leaders of the 2nd Platoon-- consisting of two dollar privates. Various other divisions reported similar problems.

The American public responded with shock and also despair as they had fourteen months earlier on Tarawa. The discussion about the high expense of forcibly confiscating an enemy island surged in the press while the battle was being dealt with. The Marine Corps released only one declaration on February 22 about detailed fight losses throughout the fighting. They reported casualties of virtually 5,000.

William Randolph Hearst was a very early fan of the MacArthur for President campaign. Hearst ran a front-page editorial in the San Francisco Examiner condemning the terrible Marine losses on bad techniques: "it's the same point that took place on Saipan and Tarawa." The editorial advised for the elevation of General MacArthur to superior commander of the Pacific, because: "HE SAVES THE LIVES OF HIS OWN MEN."

One hundred off-duty Marines disagreed as well as stormed the offices of the inspector and demanded an apology. The Hearst editorial had actually already obtained wide play. Numerous families of guys combating in the Pacific were sent the cuttings. Militaries obtained these in the mail while the battling still raged on Iwo-- an unwelcome impact for spirits.

FDR, a professional in adjusting public opinion, maintained a lid on the outcry by emphasizing the troops' sacrifice as signified by Joe Rosenthal's Suribachi flag-raising. While this picture was already popular, Roosevelt made it the main logo of the Seventh War Bond Drive. He purchased the 6 flag raisers be reassigned house to increase morale, yet 3 out of those six guys had actually currently been eliminated in the battling on Iwo Jima.

The Joint Chiefs studied Iwo's losses. No one questioned the objective: Iwo Jima was an island that needed to be safeguarded to introduce a reliable calculated bombing project. The island could not have been bypassed or leapfrogged. There was proof the Joint Chiefs considered using poison gas throughout the preparation phase. Neither the US neither Japan had actually signed the worldwide cessation on toxin gas, and also there were no civilians on the island. The United States had actually stocked mustard gas coverings in the Pacific Theater. He shot down the concept when FDR checked out the record. He openly specified that the United States would certainly never ever make very first use toxin gas. This left the landing force without other alternative however a frontal amphibious attack against the most heavily fortified island the United States had actually ever before dealt with.

The capture of Iwo Jima gave other strategic and also symbolic benefits. Marines raised the flag over Suribachi the same day MacArthur entered Manila. The identical captures of the Philippines as well as Suribachi were adhered to instantly by the intrusion of Okinawa-- speeding up the rate of the war and also bringing it finally to Japan's front door. These 3 projects proved to the Japanese command that the Allies had the capacity as well as will to overwhelm also one of the most resolutely protected islands. Honshu as well as Kyushu would be next.

The capture of Iwo Jima supplied prompt benefits to the calculated bombing project. Marines dealing with on the island were reminded of this mission repetitively as maimed B-29s flew in from Honshu. Rebuilding as well as protecting Iwo's airfields boosted the operating array haul and survival rate of the big bombing planes. The month-to-month tonnage of high explosives went down on Japan by the B-29s based in the Marianas enhanced eleven-fold in March alone. On April 7, eighty P-51 Mustangs removed from Iwo, accompanying the B- 29s bombing the Nakajima aircraft engine plant in Tokyo.

The wonderful worth of Iwo's airfields was that they can be made use of as emergency landing fields. By war's end, 2,252 B-29s made required touchdowns

on Iwo. These compelled touchdowns included 24,765 trip crewmen. Many of these males would certainly have died mixed-up without Iwo's safe haven. According to one B-29 pilot: "whenever I came down on that island, I said thanks to God for the men that passed away and battled for it."
General Kuribayashi confirmed to be one of the most proficient field leaders the Marines had actually ever dealt with. His professional understanding of simpleness as well as economic situation of force made optimal use Iwo's powerful terrain. He deployed his mortars and weapons with fantastic ability as well as commanded his soldiers with an iron will-- throughout. He was a rationalist. With no hope of marine or air superiority, he knew he was doomed from the beginning. Allied pressures took 5 weeks to breach every strong point and eradicate his forces on the island.
Iwo Jima was the pinnacle of Allied aquatic capabilities in the Pacific. The large magnitude of intending the assault as well as sustaining the touchdown forces made Operation Detachment an enduring model of detailed planning as well as violent execution. The aspect of shock was not readily available. The speed of the landing pressure and the sturdiness with which attack units stood up to the withering batteries impressed the adversary defenders.
Colonel Wornham of the 27th Marines said: "The Iwo touchdown was the embodiment of whatever we 'd found out throughout the years about aquatic attacks. Bad as the enemy fire got on D-Day, there were no records of 'Issue doubtful.'".
Colonel Galer contrasted his Guadalcanal experience to the battle on Iwo: "after that, it was can we hold? On Iwo, the concern was just, when can we get this over?".
While the ship-to-shore attacks were impressive, the actual degree of aquatic performance was seen in the large, sustained logistical assistance which flowed over the treacherous beaches. Marines had all the ammunition and weapon refills they needed all the time. They likewise had lots of less evident needs that marked this battle in different ways than its predecessors. Marines on Iwo had adequate amounts of whole blood, many given away 2 weeks in advance, flown in, cooled, and always readily available.
Militaries had mail telephone call, tidy water, radio batteries, fresh-baked bread, and premade interment pens. The Iwo Jima operation was a design of interservice participation. Marine and Navy groups operated efficiently with each other. When a flotilla of tiny LCI warships fearlessly struck the seaside protection weapons to shield, the Navy made the respect of the Marines on D -

2 the Navy and Marine frogmen. Militaries appreciated the contributions of the Coast Guard, Army, Red Cross, as well as ingrained battle correspondents; all cooperated the anguish as well as magnificence of this battle.

The United States Military inhabited Iwo Jima till 1968, when territory was transferred back to Japan. Seventy-seven years later, the island remains a military-only island. It is no longer a baren moonscape, however covered in abundant greenery, yet two facets of this fight are still controversial: inadequate preliminary bombardment and also the choice to use bit-by-bit replacements as opposed to organized units to strengthen the attack forces. Both choices were made in the context of several contending factors and also were made by seasoned commanders in excellent faith. Iwo Jima's greatest cost was the loss of many battle experts while taking the island. While this battle developed a new generation of professional heroes amongst the survivors, lots of pleased regiments experienced disastrous losses.

Those expert programs had actually already been designated as crucial landing force parts in the Japanese home islands assault-- these losses had severe prospective ramifications. It may have been these factors that affected Holland Smith's undesirable choice to withhold the 3rd Marines from the fight.

To many tired Marines and commanders combating on Iwo Jima, Holland Smith's choice to keep the 3rd Marines was unforgivable-- after that and now. But whatever his defects, General Holland Smith likely recognized amphibious warfare far better than anybody at the time.

According to Holland Smith: "We had no hope of shock, either critical or tactical. There was little possibility for tactical initiative. The whole procedure was battled on essentially the enemy's terms. The toughness, conduct, and personality of the adversary's protection needed a significant infiltration of his prepared positions in the facility of the Motoyama Plateau and a subsequent decrease of his placements in tough terrain sloping to the shore on the flanks.

" The surface and dimension of the island prevented any Force Beachhead Line. It was a one-phase and also one-tactic procedure. From the time the involvement was joined up until the objective was completed, it was a frontal assault preserved with ruthless pressure by a superior pressure in supporting arms versus a placement fortified to the optimum functional intent.

" We Americans of a subsequent generation in the profession of arms discover it hard to think of a sustained amphibious assault under these problems. In some aspects, the battling on Iwo Jima took the features of the Marines.

dealing with in France in 1918. We sensed the dramatization duplicated every early morning on Iwo Jima after the prep fires raised, when the rifleman, designers, corpsman, fire storage tank crews, and armored bulldozers somehow located the perseverance to vacate again into The Meatgrinder or Death Valley. Few of us today can research the defenses, examine the after-action reports, or walk that busted ground without experiencing a feeling of respect for the males that battled and won that impressive fight.".

While the combating was surging on Iwo, Admiral Nimitz stated: "Among the Americans serving on Iwo Jima, unusual valiance was a typical merit." This line was chiseled right into the base of Felix de Weldon's gigantic bronze sculpture of the Suribachi flag-raising.

On Iwo, Twenty-two Marines, 4 Navy corpsmen, and also one LCI skipper were granted the Medal of Honor for valor throughout the battle-- half were awarded posthumously.

General Erskine placed the Allied sacrifices right into viewpoint during his statements at the commitment of the 3rd Marine Division's Cemetery on Iwo Jima: "Our success was never ever in doubt. Its price was. What was in doubt, in all of our minds, was whether there would certainly be any of us left to devote this cemetery at the end. Or if the last Marine would pass away knocking senseless the last Japanese artilleryman."

ICONIC FLAG RAISING

There were 2 flags elevated over Mount Suribachi-- but not at the exact same time. On the morning of February 23, 1945, (D +4) Captain Dave Severance,.

Company E Commander, 2/28 Marines, purchased Lieutenant Harold

Schrier to take a patrol and also set up an American flag on the top of Mount Suribachi.

Team Sergeant Lou Lowery, a Leatherneck publication photographer, signed up with the patrol. After a short firefight, the 54" x 28" flag was attached to a piece of pipe found at the ridge of the mountain and was raised. This was the flag-raising that Staff Sergeant Lowery photographed. This flag was too small to be seen from the coastline below, and also an additional Marine went on board LST 779 to get a larger flag. Then, a 2nd patrol took this flag approximately the top of Suribachi, accompanied by AP digital photographer Joe Rosenthal.

In an interview after the war, Rosenthal claimed: "my finding that image remained in all respects accidental. When I succeeded of the hill, I stood in a decline simply below the crest of the hill with Sergeant Bill Genaust, a motion picture cameraman (later eliminated on Iwo Jima). We enjoyed a group of 5 Marines and a Navy corpsman attach the brand-new flag to another item of pipeline. I turned, and also out of the corner of my eye, I saw the 2nd flag being elevated. I turned my cam around and also held it up until I can think where the peak of the activity was and afterwards took the shot.".

Some individuals accused Rosenthal's second flag-raising photo of being positioned. According to Rosenthal's postwar interview: "had I posed that shot, I would, obviously, have actually ruined it. I would've made them transform their heads so they might be identified, as well as absolutely nothing like the existing image would certainly have resulted. This photo and also what it suggested to me-- as well as it has a significance to me-- needs to be strange only to me.

" I can still see blood diminishing the sand. I can see those dreadful, difficult placements to take in a frontal assault on such an island, where the batteries opposing you were not just surprised up before you but likewise stood around you as you came onto land. The remarkable scenario they were in prior to they ever before reached that optimal. If a picture can advise us of the sacrifices these kids made-- then that was what made the photo important-- not the guy that took it.".

Rosenthal took eighteen photographs that day. Later, he went down to the coastline to create captions for his untaught movie packs and, with various other photographers on the island, sent his film out to the offshore command vessel. They were flown to Guam, where the pictures were refined and censored. Rosenthal's pictures showed up on Guam before Lowery's as well as were processed and sent out to the states for distribution. Rosenthal's flag-raising photo turned into one of one of the most famous pictures ever taken in the war--.or in any kind of battle.

ALLIED COMMANDERS

Four professional Marine generals led the assault on Iwo Jima. Every one of these generals got the Distinguished Solution Medal for passionate fight management in this epic battle.

Major General Harry Schmidt was fifty-eight years of ages when he was on
Iwo Jima. He would certainly already served thirty-six years in the Marine
Corps. Born as well as raised in Holdrege, Nebraska, he attended the Nebraska
Normal College. His expeditionary tasks maintained him from serving in
World War I, however Schmidt saw considerable tiny device action in China,
the Philippines, Guam, Mexico, Nicaragua, and also Cuba.
Schmidt went to the Army Command and General Staff College and the
Marine Corps Field Officer's Course. During World War II, General Schmidt
regulated the 4th Marine Division at Roi-Namur as well as in Saipan before
thinking command of the V Amphibious Corps at the Tinian landing.
On Iwo Jima, he commanded the biggest force of Marines ever before

committed to a solitary battle. According to Schmidt: "it was the greatest honor of my life."

* * *

Major General Graves B. Erskine was forty-seven years old on Iwo Jima, and one of the youngest major generals in the Marine Corps. He'd already served twenty-eight years on active duty by then. A native of Columbia, Louisiana, he received a Marine Corps commission after graduating from Louisiana State University.

Erskine immediately deployed to France for duty in World War I. He served as a platoon commander in the 6th Marines and saw combat at Chateau-Thierry, Soissons, St. Mihiel, and Belleau Wood. He was wounded twice and awarded the Silver Star. He served in China, Cuba, Nicaragua, Santo Domingo, and Haiti in the interwar period.

In World War II, Erskine was Chief of Staff to General Holland Smith during the Marianas, Marshalls, Gilberts, and Aleutians campaigns. He took command of the 3rd Marine Division in October 1944.

Major General Clifton B. Cates was fifty-one years old at Iwo Jima. He'd served the last twenty-eight years in the Marine Corps. Cates was one of the rare Marine general officers who had held a combat command at the platoon, company, battalion, regiment, and division levels in his career.

Cates was born in Tiptonville, Tennessee, and graduated from the University of Tennessee. In World War I, he served as a junior officer in the 6th Marines at Blanc Mont, Soissons, Belleau Wood, and St. Mihiel. He was awarded two Silver Stars, the Navy Cross, and a Purple Heart for his service and wounds.

In the interwar years, he served at sea and in China. In World War II, he commanded the 1st Marines at Guadalcanal and the 4th Marine Division at Tinian. Three years after Iwo Jima, General Clifton Cates became the 19th Commandant of the Marine Corps.

* * *

Major General Keller E. Rockey was fifty-six years old on Iwo Jima and a thirty-one-year veteran of the Marine Corps. A native of Columbia City, Indiana, he graduated from Gettysburg College and studied at Yale. Like his fellow division commanders, Rockey served in France in World War I and was awarded the Navy Cross as a junior officer in the 5th Marines at Chateau-Thierry.

He earned a second Navy Cross for heroic service in Nicaragua. He also served in Haiti and had two years of sea duty. After spending the first years of World War II at Marine Corps Headquarters in Washington, in February

1944, General Rockey took command of the 5th Marine Division and prepared them for their first and last great battle of the war.

Three other brigadier generals played a considerable role in the amphibious seizure of Iwo Jima:

- Leo Hermle, Assistant Division Commander of the 5th Marine Division.
- Franklin Hart, Assistant Division Commander of the 4th Marine Division.
- William Rogers, Corps Chief of Staff.

GENERAL KURIBAYASHI

According to Colonel Chambers, Battalion Commander of the 3/25 Marines, whose four days on Iwo Jima resulted in a Purple Heart and a Medal of Honor: "On Iwo, their smartest general commanded. This man did not believe in the banzai business. He ordered each Jap to kill ten Marines—and for a while, they made their quotas."

Chambers was referring to Lieutenant General Kuribayashi, Commander of the *Ogasawara Army Group* and Commanding General of the *109th Division*. Tadamichi Kuribayashi was fifty-three years old on Iwo. He was from the Nagano Prefecture and served the Emperor as a cavalry officer since graduating from the Military Academy in 1914. Kuribayashi spent several years as a junior officer posted to the Japanese embassies in Canada and the United States. During the war in Asia, Kuribayashi commanded a cavalry regiment in Manchuria and a brigade in northern China. Later he served as Chief of Staff for the *Twenty-third Army* during the capture of Hong Kong.

After returning from China, the Emperor chose Kuribayashi to command the *Imperial Guards Division* in Tokyo. When Saipan fell in June 1944, he was assigned to command the defense of Iwo Jima.

Kuribayashi was a realist. He believed the crude airstrips on Iwo were a liability for the Empire. They provided nuisance raids against the B-29s but would undoubtedly draw attention from Allied strategic planners. The Iwo Jima airfields in Allied hands would pose a terrible threat to Japan.

Kuribayashi knew he had only two options: blow up the entire island or defend it to the death. Blowing up the entire island would be impractical, so he adopted a radical defensive policy. His troops would not use the suicidal banzai nor linear water's edge tactics used in previous island battles. This caused a massive controversy at the highest levels—Imperial headquarters even asked the Nazis for advice on how to repel American invasions.

While Kuribayashi made some compromises with his forces on the island, he fired eighteen senior army officers, including his chief of staff. Those who remained would implement Kuribayashi's policy to the letter.

The general knew he was doomed without air and naval support. Still, he proved to be a tenacious and resourceful commander. His only tactical error was in authorizing sector commanders to engage the Allied task force covering the UDT operations on D -2. This gift revealed to the gunners the masked batteries which would have slaughtered more of the landing force assault waves on D-Day.

Controversial Japanese accounts reported Kuribayashi committed *Seppuku* (Japanese ritual suicide) in his cave near Kitano point on March 23, 1945—the thirty-third day of battle. General

Holland Smith said: "of all our adversaries in the Pacific, Kuribayashi was the most redoubtable. Let's hope the Japs don't have any more like him."

JAPANESE SPIGOT MORTAR

One of the deadliest weapons faced on Iwo Jima was the 320mm spigot mortar. These gigantic defensive weapons were placed and operated by the Imperial Japanese Army's *20th Independent Mortar Battalion*.

The mortar tube had a small muzzle cavity. It rested on a steel base plate supported by a wooden platform. Unlike typical mortars, this five-foot-long projectile was placed over the tube instead of dropping down the barrel.   The mortar shell's diameter was thirteen inches, while the tube was only a little more than ten inches wide.

This weapon hurled a 675-pound shell over 1,500 yards. The range was adjusted by varying the powder charge, while deflection changes were accomplished by brute force: pushing and shoving the base platform. Although tubes only held out for six rounds, enough shells were lobbed onto Allied positions to make a lasting impression.

A rifleman in the 28th Marines referred to it as "The Screaming Jesus." Most Marines had a healthy respect for the mortar. General Robert Cushman, who commanded the 2/9 Marines on Iwo Jima (later becoming the 25th Commandant of the Marine Corps), recalled the inaccuracy and terror of the tumbling projectiles: "you could see it coming. But you never knew where the hell it was going to come down."

IWO'S AIR SUPPORT

For a few memorable moments before the D-Day landing, the Marines' vision of an integrated air-ground assault team became a reality. As assault troops neared the beach in their tracked amphibian vehicles, dozens of F4U Corsairs swept in and paved the way with rockets and machine-gun fire. According to one Marine: "it was magnificent."

Unfortunately, the Marine fighter squadrons on Iwo Jima that morning came from the fast attack carriers of Task Force 58, not the amphibious task force. Three days later, Task Force 58 left for good in pursuit of more strategic targets. Following that, Navy and Army Air Force pilots provided support for the landing force fighting ashore. Sustained close air support of amphibious forces by Marine air was (once again) postponed for some future combat proving ground.

Other Marine aviation units contributed to the capture of Iwo Jima. One of the first to see action was VMB 612 (Marine Bombing Squadron) out of Saipan. Flight crews on PBJ Mitchell medium bombers ran long-range nightly rocket attacks against enemy ships trying to resupply. These nightly raids, along with the Navy's submarine interdictions, slashed the amount of ammunition and fortifications (mostly barbed wire) delivered to the enemy before the invasion.

Pilots and aerial spotters from Marine observation squadrons flew in from escort carriers or were launched from the infamous *LST 776's* slingshot. These crews played a crucial role in spotting enemy artillery and mortar positions and reporting them.

Marine transport aircraft based in the Marianas delivered critical combat cargo to the island at the height of the battle. Marines relied on aerial delivery before the landing force could establish a fully functional beachhead. On D +1, marine transport squadrons airdropped critically needed machine gun parts, mortar shells, and blood plasma within the lines. On March 3, Colonel Malcolm Mackay landed the first Marine transport aircraft on the island—a Curtiss Commando R5C loaded with ammunition. The three other Marine squadrons followed and brought in much-needed supplies and evacuated the wounded.

On March 8, Marine Torpedo Bomber Squadron 224 flew in from Tinian and took responsibility for day and night anti-submarine patrols. Colonel Vernon Megee had the honor of commanding the first Landing Force Air Support Control Unit (a landmark in the evolution of amphibious combat).

Megee came ashore on D +5 with General Schmidt, but the offloading process was still in such shambles that it took five days to gather communication jeeps. This did not deter Megee. He "borrowed" gear and moved inland to coordinate the Air Liaison Parties. He persuaded Navy pilots to use bigger bombs and listened to the assault commanders' complaints.

McGee's work in training and employing Army P-51 Mustang pilots was masterful. Kuribayashi transmitted to Tokyo "lessons learned" in   defending against the Allied amphibious assault during the battle. One of his messages said: "the enemy's air control is strong. At least thirty aircraft flew ceaselessly from early morning to night over this very small island."

SHERMAN ZIPPO TANKS

For many Marines on Iwo Jima, the Sherman M4A3—with the Mark I flamethrower—was the most effective weapon employed in the battle.

On Iwo, Marines had come a long way with the tactical use of fire. Fifteen months earlier on Tarawa, only a handful of backpack flamethrowers were available to fight hundreds of the island's fortifications. While the assault force relied on portable flamethrowers, most Marines saw the value in marrying this technology with armored vehicles for use against the island's toughest targets.

In the Marianas, Marines modified M3A1 light tanks with the Canadian Ronson flame system to a deadly effect. But the small vehicles were vulnerable to enemy fire. On Peleliu, the 1st Marine Division mounted the improvised Mark I system on a thin skin LVT. But again, the vehicle's susceptibility to enemy fire limited the effectiveness of the system. The obvious solution was to mount the flamethrower on a tank.

Early modifications to the Shermans were made by replacing the bow machine gun with the small E4-5 mechanized flamethrower. Replacing the bow machine gun was only a minor improvement. The short-range, limited fuel supply and awkward aiming process did not compensate for losing the machine gun. Each of the three tank battalions used the E4-5-equipped Shermans on Iwo Jima.

The best solution for effective flame projection and mechanized mobility came from the Army's Chemical Warfare technicians on Hawaii before the invasion. Colonel Bill Collins, CO 5th Tank Battalion, inspired this tinkerer group to modify the Mark I flamethrower to operate within the Shermans' turret. By replacing the 75mm main gun with a look-alike launch tube, this modified system could be trained and pointed like any standard turret gun using napalm-thickened fuel. These Zippo tanks streamed 250 yards of flame for eighty seconds—a significant tactical improvement.

But the modification team only had enough time to modify eight M4A3 tanks with the Mark I flame system. The 4th and 5th Tank Battalions were each issued four. The 3rd Tank Battalion on Guam didn't receive any M4A3 Shermans nor field modifications in time for the battle on Iwo Jima. Although several of their A2 tanks kept the E4-5 system mounted in the bow.

The eight Sherman Zippo tanks were ideal against Iwo's rugged caves and concrete fortifications. The enemy was terrified of this weapon. Suicide squads of human bullets would attack flame tanks directly only to be shot down by covering forces or charred by napalm. Enemy fire took a toll on the eight flame tanks—but maintenance crews worked around the clock to   keep them in the fight.

Captain Frank Caldwell, Company Commander of the 26th Marines said: "it was a flame tank more than any other supporting arm that won this battle."

The tactical demand for flame tanks never diminished. The 5th Tank Battalion used 10,000 gallons of napalm-thickened fuel a day. When the 5th Marine Division had cornered the last Japanese defenders in "The Gorge," their final after-action report stated the flame tank was one of the weapons that caused the enemy to leave their caves and rock crevices and run for their lives.

BUCK ROGERS MEN

Provisional rocket detachments were attached to the subdivisions of the landing force on Iwo Jima. Marines had a love-hate relationship with the little rocket trucks and their brave crews. These trucks were a one-ton, four wheel drive truck modified to carry three box-shaped rocket launchers containing a dozen 4.5-inch rockets.

Crews fired a ripple of thirty-six rockets within seconds and provided a carpet of high explosives on the target. While effective and deadly, each launch drew heavy return fire from the Japanese—who dreaded the automatic artillery.

The Experimental Rocket Unit was formed in June 1943 and first deployed rail-launched barrage rockets during the fighting in the Solomons. There, heavily canopied jungles limited their efficiency. But once mounted on trucks and deployed in the Central Pacific, these rockets were deadly and effective, especially during the battle on Saipan.

Marines reinforced the trucks' tailgate to serve as a blast shield. They installed hydraulic jacks to raise and lower the launchers. Crude steel rods were welded to the bumper and dashboard to help the driver align the vehicle with the aiming stakes.

A hilly treeless Iwo proved an ideal battleground for the "Buck Rogers Men." The 1st Provisional Rocket Detachment supported the 4th and 5th Marine Divisions throughout the battle on Iwo Jima. The Buck Rogers Men fired over 30,000 rockets to support the landing force.

The Rocket Detachment landed on Red Beach on D-Day and lost one vehicle in the surf and several others to heavy enemy fire or loose sand. When the first vehicle reached its firing position intact, it launched a salvo of rockets against Japanese fortifications on the slopes of Suribachi. It detonated an enemy ammunition dump. The detachment supported the Marines advance to the summit, often launching single rockets to clear suspected enemy positions along the route.

As the fighting advanced north, the rocket launchers' short-range deep angle fire and saturation effect kept them in high demand. They were effective in defilade-to-defilade bombardments. But the distinct flashing telltale blast always caught the attention of the Japanese artillery spotters. The rocket trucks rarely remained in one place long enough to fire more than two salvos. A fast displacement was critical to their survival. Marines knew better than to stand around and wave goodbye—it was time to seek deep shelter from the counter-battery fire sure to follow.

LOGISTICAL SUPPORT

The logistical effort necessary to sustain the assault force on Iwo Jima was complex, enormous, and learned from previous lessons in Pacific amphibious operations. No other element of the emerging art of amphibious warfare had improved so greatly by the winter of 1945.

While Marines had the courage and firepower to tackle a fortress like Iwo

Jima, they would have been crippled without the available amphibious logistical support. The procedures, organizations, and concepts took years to develop. But once in place, they enabled the large-scale conquests on Iwo Jima and Okinawa.

On Iwo Jima, the 8th Field Depot was commanded by Colonel Leland Swindler. This depot served as the nucleus of shore party operations. Swindler coordinated the activities of all shore party operations. The logistical support on Iwo was well-conceived and executed. Liaison teams from the 8th Field Depot accompanied the 4th and 5th Divisions ashore. On D +3, field depot units came ashore, took over the unloading, and continued without interruption.

Every imaginable method of delivering combat cargo ashore was used. This involved "hot cargo," carried in by the assault waves. Hot cargo was preloaded in on assault waves or floating dumps. This experimental use of one-shot preloaded amphibious trailers, Wilson drums, and a general loading and unloading would be known to future generations as the "assault follow-on echelon."

Aerial delivery was first by parachute and then via transports landing on the captured runways. The Marine/Navy team experimented with the use of armored bulldozers and sleds loaded with hinged matting delivered by assault waves to clear wheeled vehicles stuck in the soft, volcanic sand. Despite fearsome obstacles: heavy surf, dangerous undertows, foul weather, and formidable enemy fire—the system worked. The combat cargo flowed in and kept casualties and salvaged equipment flowing out.

The occasional shortages were often the result of the Marines meeting a more robust defensive garrison than initially expected. Urgent calls for more demolitions, grenades, mortar illumination rounds, and blood plasma were common. Transport squadrons delivered many of these critical items directly from the Mariana Islands fleet bases.

The field medical support on Iwo was a model of detailed planning and flexible application. Marines received immediate medical attention from their corpsmen and surgeons. But the system from hospitals to grave registration was mind boggling to some of the older veterans. Moderately wounded Marines received full hospital treatment and rehabilitation—often returning directly to their units—this preserved some of the swiftly decreasing combat experience levels in the frontline outfits. The more seriously wounded were stabilized, evacuated, and treated in offshore hospital ships or taken by air to

Guam.

Marines fired an extraordinary half-million artillery rounds to support the assault units. Many rounds were lost when the 5th Marine Division's ammo dump blew up. But the flow never stopped. The shore party used LVTs and amphibious trucks for a fast offloading of ammunition ships dangerously exposed to enemy gunners. Marines helped the shore party hustle munitions onshore and into the neediest hands.

Colonel James Hittle of the 3rd Division (the reserve landing force) shook his head at the "crazy quilt" logistics adopted because of Iwo's geography. Hittle "appropriated" a transport plane and made regular runs to Guam—returning with fresh beef, beer, and mail. Colonel Hittle sent his transport quartermaster out to sea in an LVT full of war souvenirs to trade for bread, eggs, and fresh fruit.

Hittle was amazed at the density of troops funneled onto the small island: "at one point, we had over 60,000 men occupying less than three and a half miles of broken terrain." He directed Marine engineers to dig a well near the beach for a freshwater distilling plant. Instead of a saltwater source, engineers discovered steaming mineral water heated by Suribachi's dormant volcano.

Hittle moved the distilling site, and this spot became a hot shower facility —one of the most popular places on the island.

* * *

Building a relationship with my readers is one of the best things about writing. I occasionally send out emails with details on new releases and special offers. If you'd like to join my free readers group and never miss a new release, <u>just tap here</u> and I'll add you to the list.

After a long campaign of island hopping, the Allies planned to use Kadena Air Base on Okinawa as a base for Operation Downfall, the planned invasion of the Japanese home islands. This battle was also known as "typhoon of steel" [English translation], because of the ferocity of the fighting, the intensity of kamikaze attacks and the sheer numbers of Allied ships and armored vehicles that assaulted the island.

This narrative recounts the invasion of Okinawa in vivid, gritty detail. Explore the fascinating feats of strategy, planning, and bravery, handing the Allies what would eventually become a victory over the Pacific Theater and an end to Imperialist Japanese expansion.

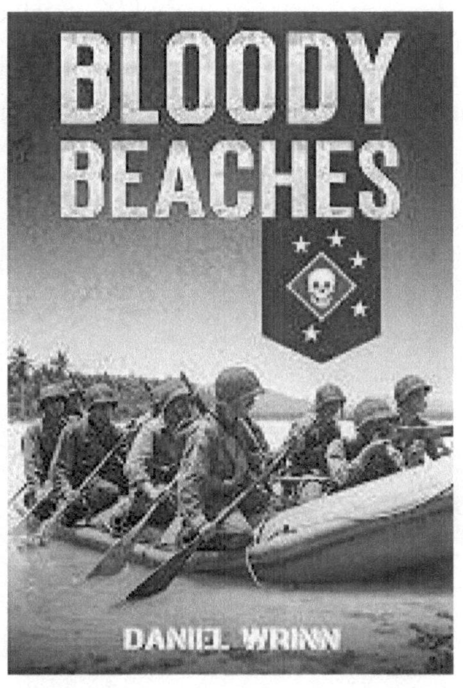

<u>BLOODY BEACHES : MARINE RAIDERS IN WORLD WAR II</u>

"Great book for Marines, former Marines and history buffs!" – Reader

A powerful account of the Marine Raiders during World War II

Marine Raiders were special operations forces established during the Pacific campaign to conduct amphibious light infantry warfare. "Edson's" Raiders of 1st Marine Raider Battalion and "Carlson's" Raiders of 2nd Marine Raider Battalion were the first US special operations forces to form and see combat during World War II.

Despite the original intent for Raiders to serve in a special operations capacity, most combat operations saw the Raiders employed as conventional infantry. This, combined with the resentment within the rest of the Marine Corps that the Raiders were an "elite force within an elite force," led to the original Raider units being disbanded.

This narrative recounts the story of the Marine Raiders in vivid, gritty detail. Explore the fascinating feats of strategy, planning, and bravery, handing the Allies what would eventually become a victory over the Pacific Theater and an end to Imperialist Japanese expansion.

<u>WORLD WAR II PACIFIC: BATTLES AND CAMPAIGNS FROM GUADALCANAL TO OKINAWA 1942-1945</u>

"A brisk and compelling game changer for the historiography of the Pacific Theater in World War II." – Reader

An enlightening glimpse into nine battles and campaigns during the Pacific War Allied offensive.

Each of these momentous operations were fascinating feats of strategy, planning, and bravery, handing the Allies what would eventually become a victory over the Pacific Theater and an end to Imperialist Japanese expansion.

Operation Watchtower, a riveting exploration of the spark that set off the Allied offensive in the Pacific islands, detailing the grueling struggle for the island of Guadalcanal and its vital strategic position.

Operation Galvanic, an incredible account of the battle for the Tarawa Atoll and base that would give them a steppingstone into the heart of Japanese-controlled waters.

Operation Backhander, a gripping retelling of the war for Cape Gloucester, New Guinea, and the Bismarck Sea.

Battle for Saipan, Marines stormed the beaches with a goal of gaining a crucial air base from which the US could launch its new long-range B-29 bombers directly at Japan's home islands.

Invasion of Tinian, is the incredible account of the assault on Tinian. Located just under six miles southwest of Saipan. This was the first use of napalm and the "shore to shore" concept.

Recapture of Guam, a gripping narrative about the liberation of the Japanese-held island of Guam, captured by the Japanese in 1941 during one of the first Pacific campaigns of the War.

Operation Stalemate, Marines landed on the island of Peleliu, one of the Palau Islands in the Pacific, as part of a larger operation to provide support for General MacArthur, who was preparing to invade the Philippines.

Operation Detachment, the battle of Iwo Jima was a major offensive in World War II. The Marine invasion was tasked with the mission of capturing airfields on the island for use by P-51 fighters.

Operation Iceberg, the invasion and ultimate victory on Okinawa was the largest amphibious assault in the Pacific Theater. It was also one of the bloodiest battles in the Pacific, lasting ninety-eight days.

This gripping narrative sheds light on these often-overlooked facets of WWII, providing students, history fans, and World War II buffs alike with a captivating breakdown of the history and combat that defined the ultimate victory of US forces in the Pacific.

REFERENCES

Alexander, Colonel Joseph. "'In for One Hell of a Time': Bloody Sacrifice at the Battle of Iwo Jima." HistoryNet.com and World War II magazine. HistoryNet.com and World War II magazine, February 2000.

Allen, Robert E. *The First Battalion of the 28th Marines on Iwo Jima: a Day-by-Day History from Personal Accounts and Official Reports, with Complete Muster Rolls*. McFarland, 1999.

"Amphibious Operations: Capture of Iwo Jima." Naval History and Heritage Command, October 23, 2019.

Antill, Peter D. "The Battle for Iwo Jima." History of War, April 6, 2001.

Bradley, James, and Ron Powers. *Flags of Our Fathers*. New York: Bantam Books, 2006.

Bradley, James. *Flyboys: a True Story of American Courage*. Boston: Little, Brown, 2003.

Buell, Hal. *Uncommon Valor, Common Virtue: Iwo Jima and the Photograph That Captured America*. New York, NY: Berkley, 406AD.

Burrell, Robert S. *The Ghosts of Iwo Jima*. College Station: Texas A&M

University Press, 2006.

Hammel, Eric M. *Iwo Jima: Portrait of a Battle: United States Marines at War in the Pacific*. St. Paul, MN: Zenith Press, 2006.

Hearn, Chester G. *Sorties into Hell: The Hidden War on Chichi Jima*. Guilford, CT: Lyons Press, 2005.

HistoricalResources. "Ivo Jima Maps - February 19, 1945–March 26, 1945." Historical Resources About The Second World War RSS, September 15, 2008.

Horie, Yoshitaka, Robert D. Eldridge, and Charles W. Tatum. *Fighting Spirit: The Memoirs of Major Yoshitaka Horie and the Battle of Iwo Jima*. Annapolis, MD: Naval Institute Press, 2011.

Kindersley, Dorling. *World War II: The Definitive Visual History*. New York: DK Publishing, 2009.

Salomon, Henry. *Victory at Sea Volume 23: Target Suribachi*. United States of America: The National Broadcasting Company, 1954.

Shively, John C. *The Last Lieutenant: A Foxhole View of the Epic Battle for Iwo Jima*. Bloomington: Indiana University Press, 2006.

Sperling, Milton. *To the Shores of Iwo Jima*. United States of America: United States Navy and United States Marine Corps, 1945.

Toll, Ian W. *TWILIGHT OF THE GODS: War in the Western Pacific, 1944-1945*. S.l.: W W NORTON, 2020.

Veronee, Marvin D. *A Portfolio of Photographs: Selected to Illustrate the Setting for My Experience in the Battle of Iwo Jima, World War II, Pacific Theater, as a Naval Gunfire Liaison Officer with the First Battalion, 28th Marines, 19 February-26 March 1945*. Quantico: Visionary Pub., 2001.

Wells, Keith. *Give Me Fifty Marines Not Afraid to Die: Iwo Jima*. Abilene, TX: Produced by Quality Publications, 1995.

Wheeler, Richard. *Iwo*. Annapolis, MD: Naval Institute Press, 1994.

World War 2 Pictures. "Iwo Jima Pictures." WW2-Pictures.com, April 16, 2010.

Wright, Derrick. *Iwo Jima 1945: The Marines Raise the Flag On Mount Suribachi*. Oxford: Osprey Publishing Ltd, 2004.

"Breaking the Cycle of Iwo Jima Mythology: A Strategic Study of Operation Detachment." *The Journal of Military History* 68, no. 4 (October 2004)

The Battle for Iwo Jima 1945. Stroud: Sutton, 2006.

"'Rare Photos of the Battle of Iwo Jima from the U.S. National Archives and the Department of Defense, USMC.'" Awesome Stories. Accessed June 2021.